Monsters in the Closet

Monsters in the Closet

*Exposing Real Threats to Children
and Teenagers Within the Home*

Adam Butler

RESOURCE *Publications* • Eugene, Oregon

MONSTERS IN THE CLOSET
Exposing Real Threats to Children and Teenagers Within the Home

Copyright © 2020 Adam Butler. All rights reserved. Except for brief quotations in critical publications or reviews, no part of this book may be reproduced in any manner without prior written permission from the publisher. Write: Permissions, Wipf and Stock Publishers, 199 W. 8th Ave., Suite 3, Eugene, OR 97401.

Resource Publications
An Imprint of Wipf and Stock Publishers
199 W. 8th Ave., Suite 3
Eugene, OR 97401

www.wipfandstock.com

PAPERBACK ISBN: 978-1-7252-8446-3
HARDCOVER ISBN: 978-1-7252-8445-6
EBOOK ISBN: 978-1-7252-8447-0

Manufactured in the U.S.A.   09/15/20

*To Mom and Dad: Thank you for instilling
in me a desire for God's Word*

Contents

Preface | ix
Introduction: Monsters Are Real | xi

Part 1: Pornography

Chapter 1: Porn is Not About Sex | 3
Chapter 2: Porn Hurts Women | 8
Chapter 3: Porn Hurts Children | 13
Chapter 4: Porn Affects Our Desires | 17
Chapter 5: The Prevalence of Pornography | 24
Chapter 6: What Can I Do? | 29

Part 2: Media

Chapter 7: Liars | 39
Chapter 8: Music | 43
Chapter 9: Social Media | 50
Chapter 10: Demons and Suicide Games | 65

Part 3: Indoctrination

Chapter 11: Attack on Christianity | 73
Chapter 12: Abortion | 76
Chapter 13: Sexuality | 86

Conclusion | 101

Appendix: Answers to Common Objections/Questions | 107
Bibliography | 115

Preface

I HAVE WORKED WITH and ministered to students in youth ministry for several years. My heart for them has only grown as I have gotten more involved and started reading and learning more about trends within youth culture.

This book started as a research project focusing strictly on the topic of pornography. I started doing extensive research into the effects of porn on both young and old people, the realities and horrors of the porn industry, and the prevalence of porn within American culture. Eventually, my research led me to discover the connections between porn and the sexualization of the culture. Naturally, this led to further reading and study on topics of the like. Eventually, I found myself writing a draft for an entire book covering what I had discovered—the dangers of the internet, media, and even the education system of secular America are much closer than we may be inclined to think.

Some of what I found was particularly shocking, having been raised in a conservative, Christian home, home schooled almost entirely until high school, and holding fast to Biblical values all the way. The culture shock was real for me when I first attended public school as a freshman. After getting involved in student ministry shortly after high school, the realities of what students are exposed to on a regular basis became even more clear.

The point of this book is not to make a case against an issue, though I will provide Biblical responses to certain arguments. Books like that have already been written, and I have recommended many of the ones I have found most helpful. The point of this book is to expose some of the most dangerous and false ideas and content being fed to children and teenagers. Many of us have put blinders on to the culture around us, often inadvertently, and have missed the revolutions taking place in the lives of children. They are the targets because their minds are the easiest to shape. There are real monsters which have snuck into the home and are preying on young people. This book should serve as an expository work to just how easy it is to let them in your home, and what you can do to get them out. We must remove the blinders and replace them with the lens of a Biblical worldview, so that we may be better equipped to evaluate the world around us that we will inevitably be challenged and even attacked by at some point.

Some of what I have included in this book may be disturbing, especially if you had a background such as mind and are not used to being awakened by the stark shift in culture which we are currently experiencing. I do believe these are necessary facts to shed light on, however, as without the knowledge of their existence, we may not know how to react, much less that we ought to react to begin with.

As I will argue, there is an undercurrent linking everything I address in this book—the influence of the enemy. Satan's grip on society grows tighter and tighter as we await the final days. I pray that as you read this, it will encourage you to remain faithful to God's Word amidst an ever-increasingly hostile world. We as followers of Christ are the light of the world, called to be salt and light. So, use this book as a tool to inform you of the new tactics of the enemy, and how you can stand firm on the front lines of this spiritual battle.

Introduction

Monsters Are Real

"Mommy, Daddy, can you check my closet for *monsters?*" Many children have an irrational fear of monsters while growing up. Interestingly, even without having been exposed to horror films, many kids still fear a scary being lurking in the darkness of the closet, or perhaps under the bed. Why? They are scared of the unknown. Who is to say there *isn't* a monster in the closet? That is why they often ask parents to check before bed.

What if I told you that fears like this are not so irrational after all? Obviously, I am not talking about big hairy monsters like in the movie Monsters Inc. I am talking about a different kind of monster that could be lurking in your home whether you know it or not. In fact, I am referring to very real threats that could be facing your child right now. Very real monsters that have one thing in common: they may be available to your child by the touch of a finger.

The internet is one of the most important technological advances in human history, but also one of the most dangerous. It is a gateway to pornography, predators, media lies, indoctrination, and even, as I will argue, a root of demonic activity. These are the modern monsters that may be sneaking around in your

INTRODUCTION: MONSTERS ARE REAL

child's bedroom late at night. The difference between these virtual monsters and the big, hairy monsters that kids fear is that *these monsters are real*.

"What am I allowing my child to be exposed to?" Is demonic activity real and if so, *is it in my home?* How accessible is pornography, and how big of a threat is it? What are the effects of porn exposure at a young age? What are the effects of media/information overload? *What can I do?*

In this book, I will seek to evaluate some of the major threats that are facing children and teenagers right now as you are reading this. I will look at them through the lens of a Biblical, Gospel-centered worldview, and I will attempt to answer these questions to the best of my ability. I will also provide resources for addressing some of these topics. Parents are the gatekeepers of the household; it is their responsibility to discern what their children are being exposed to. In a media-driven age, this is more important than ever.

Discipleship begins in the home. As Proverbs says, "Train up a child in the way he should go, Even when he is old he will not depart from it." (Proverbs 22:6).

Why This Matters Today

I have been working with students in ministry for several years; leading small groups, speaking, and just hanging out. In a short period of time, one of the things I have learned is that there is so much to learn. What we need to realize is that *the generational gaps are getting wider and wider.* In other words, for every new generation of people, there are new threats that older generations are having a harder time addressing. Why? Because it is so new. My generation is known as Generation Z. There are topics, trends, and issues my generation has grown up with that people one a couple of generations before me are completely blown away by. Some of them are simply cultural trends, but others have a greater impact on truth. Because we grew up with these things being considered, to some degree, "normal" or status quo, we are not fazed by them. Older generations, however, have a much more difficult time contextualizing and thus helping young people think through such things.

All that is to say it is vital to be aware of what is going on, especially in the lives of young people. As followers of Christ, we are called to be salt and light (Matthew 5:13–16) and further, to have answers (1 Peter 3:15). To do this, we must be aware.

I was a bit ashamed the other day as I was conversing with someone and trying to describe the importance of being informed. Unfortunately, I could not think of the right word; the only word that came to mind was "woke." That's what the kids are saying these days. We must be "woke," or informed, in order to know how to fight against the very real monsters of the day.

Kids have questions. Let us have answers. Let us be ready to defend what we believe and raise them up to be faithful to Christ, and not to fall into the enemy's many traps. There is a war going on, and many children are on the front lines, completely exposed.

Part 1: **Pornography**

1

Porn Is Not About Sex

I WAS AROUND 11 years old, and I vividly remember the exact video I watched. I remember the room I was in, the time of day, and the website. The video was not educational, as if to explain the process of intercourse. It was an explicit, exaggerated, almost extreme form of sex. That video was my first exposure to pornography, which I later discovered is exactly what the porn industry aims for—and this type of videography is getting even worse. It left me feeling shameful and a bit disgusted. I had rarely seen pictures of naked bodies, much less images of people having sex. Yet, I had been given a small glimpse into the multi-billion-dollar industry of perverted sex.

As it turns out, I am not alone in my experience with porn exposure; the average age a child is exposed to pornography is 11 years old.[1] With the increasing availability of pornographic content, (which I will discuss in the following pages,) I fear this age of exposure will only continue to drop. In fact, porn is where many young people are receiving their sex education. Feminist author and journalist, Naomi Wolf, after interviewing students at a large university, recounts, "It became clear that after a decade of having

---

1. For this exact statistic and others, visit https://fightthenewdrug.org/real-average-age-of-first-exposure/

access to the internet they were intimately familiar with porn, but intimacy—and the hearts of the opposite sex—were more of an elusive mystery than ever."[2]

I am not a current or recovering porn addict; even so, I hope to inform you of the truth about the industry itself and the harm it has done to women, as well as the detrimental effects porn has on the brain, marriage, sex, our desires, and society. Pornography is a real issue, and one that is destroying marriages, affecting the way people view sex, creating addicts, and becoming increasingly harmful to porn "actors."

Before we jump into the crux of the issue, I first need to define some terms. That is, we need to first establish what porn is *not* about.

Porn is *Not* About Sex

What could possibly be so harmful about looking at photos of naked people or watching videos of people having sex? What about porn video-shoots could be so harmful to the actors themselves? After all, sex is a natural part of life; it is how we bond with a spouse, share physical intimacy, and not to mention is the mechanism by which we reproduce. So, why all the "closed doors?" Why are we so secretive about our personal sex lives? There is a good reason. Sex is sacred.

The closed doors of sex are flying open more and more each day, however. It does not take much investigation to realize that media is saturated with sex. Posters, billboards, ads, movies, television shows, clothing styles, and even brands which sell products having nothing to do with sex use sex to sell their products.[3] The

---

2. Wolf, "Casual Sex," *The Sunday Times*.

3. Several years ago, the Hardee's and Carl's Jr. franchise began using models wearing scantily clad clothing and eating burgers in provocative ways in their commercials. The commercials were a hit for some, but also raised some concern among viewers and backlash for the company. Eventually, the company agreed to stop using sex to sell food—read about it here: https://www.chicagotribune.com/business/ct-carls-jr-hardees-end-sexy-advertising-20170330-story.html

reason given, as you probably have heard, is that "sex sells." In reality, however, studies have shown that sexualized advertising actually has little or no effect on whether the consumer buys the product advertised.[4] So, does sex really sell? Not according to the research. Why, then, do companies insist on sexy advertising?

The Culture of Sex

Because sex has become a part of our culture. Merriam Webster defines *culture* as "the customary beliefs, social forms, and material traits of a racial, religious, or social group," or "the set of shared attitudes, values, goals, and practices that characterizes an institution or organization." Culture varies by people-groups, but also over time. It is a moving target; that is, if we want to stay culturally "relevant," stay up to date on the cultural trends, or even make an impact on culture, we must meet the culture where it is. This is known as *contextualization*. The first thing you learn about when moving to or visiting another country, besides the language, is the culture. Any aspect of culture, however, is susceptible to abuse and perversion.

Western-American culture celebrates sex. Pornography, however, has taken what is meant to be a beautiful thing and perverted it. Porn has almost become a norm to society. Memes about watching porn are permeated throughout social media and meme websites like "iFunny." Teenagers talk about porn nonchalantly. Why?

If there is one place where sex *does* sell, it is the porn industry. Globally, porn is an estimated *$97 billion* industry, with *$12 billion* of that coming from the U.S. Typically, females are paid anywhere from $800 to $1000 for a porn video. Not surprisingly, men are generally paid significantly less than that. Why? Because the male audience of porn-watchers is significantly greater than the female audience. That is, traffic to porn sites is *72 percent male* and only *28 percent* female.

Needless to say, the porn industry is raking in a ton of money. In fact, porn sites receive more visitors each month than Netflix,

---

4. Raghuram, "Effects of Sexual Advertising," *IOSR Journal of Business Engagement* vol. 7, 6–10.

Amazon, and Twitter *combined*. Porn sites rank second place, next to YouTube, with the most monthly visitors. YouTube averages 800 million viewers every month, while porn sites average 450 million.[5]

But it was not always this way.

Only with the increase of availability and technology has the consumption of pornographic content reached all-time highs. Porn was not always as effortless to get a hold of. Though depictions of sexual intercourse have been common among cultures of even ancient times, pornography rose to popularity with erotic literature.[6] Fast forward to the rise of porn magazines, the most notable being *Playboy*. Magazines were sold in gas stations and adult entertainment sections of retail stores; consumers often had to request them by name from the check-out counter. Hence, attaining pornographic content was much more difficult (and expensive)! Of course, erotic films were popular among the adult crowd as well, though they were also a lot more out-of-reach, so to speak, and with good reason. Adult content was exclusive to the adult crowd. Then, along came the internet.

Internet porn is the primary reason the porn industry achieved such stunning success in sales and viewer traffic. However, even in the early days of internet porn, pornographic content was a lot less accessible. You had to really be searching to find what you were looking for. Now, it seems children are stumbling upon explicit content without even meaning to![7] The more accessible the internet became, the more the porn industry followed.

---

5. Kleinman, "Porn Sites," *Huffpoost*.

6. Lane, *Obscene Profits*, 11.

7. An article on *fightthenewdrug.org*, a website for awareness of the dangers of the porn industry, explains, "According to a report by CNBC, Google recently deleted 60 apps from its Google Play app store, many of them kid-themed. This was after security firm Check Point found that they contained malicious adware that could display pornographic content, trick users into installing fake "security apps," or induce them to sign up for premium SMS services." Read about it here: https://fightthenewdrug.org/google-removes-kids-apps-because-of-porn/

Today, over 5 billion people have mobile devices of some sort, over half of them being smartphones.[8] That means that over 5 billion people potentially have a free, private means of access to internet pornography. What a big change from the days of Playboy Magazine!

So, it is no wonder children are being exposed to pornography at stiflingly young ages; it has never been easier to find.

---

8. Silver, "Smartphone Ownership," *Pew Research Center.*

2

Porn Hurts Women

THERE IS A REASON that porn actors are just that—actors. The things on the screen are often not what they seem. In the film industry, everything is about the art of the movie. This is sometimes referred to as "movie magic." Not everyone can pull out a camera and make a movie; it takes a director, a cast, a videographer, editing, and countless reshoots. Essentially, the actors are at the disposal of the director if they want to get paid. That is, the director gets to decide how the scene looks and plays out. Unfortunately, pornography is no different. In fact, it is often worse.

Actors in porn shoots are often abused at the hands of the directors or their components. In this chapter, I am going to focus on specifically the female roles in porn, being that they are possibly the most susceptible to abuse and even trafficking, as we will discuss later. Female abuse in porn is nothing recent, however. Author and professor, Nancy Pearcey, discusses the root of pornography this way:

> Recent translations use the term "fornication" or "sexual immorality." But those expressions are still far too tame. The word *porneia* comes from the word meaning "to buy," and in the polytheistic literature of the day, it meant "prostitution" and "whoring." And the practice of *porneia* was at least as dehumanizing then as it is today. In

ancient Rome and Greece, a *porne* or prostitute was normally a slave. Sex slaves were often physically abused.[1]

Like I said earlier, porn is not about sex—it is about the presentation and the profit. Viewers will not be satisfied unless the video is presented right, with the correct amount of exaggerated acting. The way the industry achieves this is often not as simple as acting school, though sadly, women and men often have to attend these "sex acting" classes as well.[2] Both men and women have to learn how *not* to feel anything, in order to keep up the acting persona and fulfil the desired role. For this, they are trained to be able to withhold orgasm, the climax of sexual intimacy, in order to get through the entire shoot. They also must learn to suppress any romantic or intimate feelings toward the other actor, in order to keep with the theme of the video. While this process sounds simple (yet disturbing), it is a heartbreaking reality.

Former porn stars are often unable to establish lasting sexual relationships with people after having been involved in the porn industry for so long. In addition, porn *viewers* experience the same travesty. We will delve into the personal effects of porn later. The porn industry has hijacked the intimacy and relationship of sex and made it completely about a profitable show of extreme, brutal, and unrealistic behavior. Even so, modern culture has adopted this narrative, with a message of "Don't be boring. Be like porn stars."[3] This is the pornified culture that has been created and is still growing. A study on representations of orgasms during porn says this:

> Social representations, which appear in a variety of media, can influence the way sexual experiences are perceived and understood. While pornography is not the only medium in which orgasm is portrayed, it is the most explicit, and it is widespread and easily accessible. As such, pornography is an ideal medium for examining representations of male and female orgasm.[4]

1. Pearcey, *Love Thy Body*, 142–143.
2. Szulman, "Porn University," *Daily News*.
3. Owens, "My Rape," *Verily*.
4. Séguin, "Consuming Ecstasy," *The Journal of Sex Research*, 348–356.

What the study is claiming, rightly so, is that what is displayed in pornography then becomes what is expected in real life. As a result, men who watch porn end up expecting their partner to behave as the female role in the film. Likewise, women who watch porn expect men to behave as the actors do. The women are also left believing they should act as expressly as the female actors. When these two false expectations collide, neither the male nor female in a sexual relationship is satisfied. The porn culture has created a one-sided representation of sex.

This is especially problematic, considering the vast number of children who are exposed to sex via porn. Hence, Pearcey notes, "From childhood, young people are awash in sexual *imagery*, but sexual *intimacy* is increasingly difficult to achieve."[5]

In fact, researchers have analyzed the top 50 most viewed videos on one of the world's leading pornography websites. In the videos, 78 percent of the males achieve orgasm, while a mere 18.3 percent of women orgasm.[6] The industry is adapted to the audience which views it the most—men; they are therefore the ones who benefit the most in the scripts of the videos. The lack of mutual pleasure demonstrates the false narrative porn has created—devoid of intimacy. In fact, none of the physical and emotional intimacies which should be experienced by a couple that loves each other are displayed in porn videos. There is most often no talking (unless it involves vulgar language, often demeaning toward the partner), no romance, no cuddling, no sign of a healthy relationship at all. Instead, women are often beaten and yelled at, to which they almost always respond with pleasure.[7]

So, what? Isn't it her body, her choice? Shouldn't people be allowed to do what they want with porn? Not when that choice may be severely harmful to the woman. The problem is that women in porn are often *not* doing what they want; they are being forced into extreme scenarios, most of which they are not aware of beforehand.

---

5. Pearcey, *Love Thy Body*, 125
6. Fight the New Drug, "One-Sided Orgasms."
7. Bridges, "Aggression," *Violence Against Women*, 16(10), 1065–1085.

Porn hurts women. As mentioned before, most of what is seen on the screen is not real—it is acting. In order to keep with the theme of the film, and the theme of women in porn, women are often forced into extreme scenarios.

The following descriptions are graphic. These are real examples from actual former porn actors explaining the realities of the porn industry and how women are treated.

> "[One particular film] was the most brutal, depressing, scary scene that I have ever done. I have tried to block it out from my memory due to the severe abuse that I received during the filming. The [male performer] has a natural hatred towards women, in the sense that he has always been known to be more brutal than ever needed. I agreed to do the scene, thinking it was less beating except a punch in the head. If you noticed, [he] had worn his solid gold ring the entire time and continued to punch me with it. I actually stopped the scene while it was being filmed because I was in too much pain."

> "It was the most degrading, embarrassing, horrible thing ever. I had to shoot an interactive DVD, which takes hours and hours of shooting time, with a 104 degree fever! I was crying and wanted to leave but my agent wouldn't let me, he said he couldn't let me flake on it. I also did a scene where I was put with male talent that was on my 'no list'. I wanted to please them, so I did it. He stepped on my head [. . .] I freaked out and started bawling; they stopped filming and sent me home with reduced pay since they got some shot but not the whole scene."

> "After a year or so of that so-called 'glamorous life,' I sadly discovered that drugs and drinking were part of the lifestyle. I began to drink and party out of control—cocaine, alcohol, and ecstasy were my favorites. Before long, I turned into a person I did not want to be. After doing so many hardcore scenes, I couldn't do it anymore. I just remember being in horrible situations and experiencing extreme depression and being alone and sad."

PART 1: PORNOGRAPHY

"I got the **** kicked out of me . . . most of the girls start crying because they're hurting so bad . . . I couldn't breathe. I was being hit and choked. I was really upset and they didn't stop. They kept filming. [I asked them to turn the camera off] and they kept going."

"People in the porn industry are numb to real life and are like zombies walking around. The abuse that goes on in this industry is completely ridiculous. The way these young ladies are treated is totally sick and brainwashing. I left due to the trauma I experienced even though I was there only a short time. I hung out with a lot of people in the adult industry, everybody from contract girls to gonzo actresses. Everybody has the same problems. Everybody is on drugs. It's an empty lifestyle trying to full up a void. I became horribly addicted to heroin and crack. I overdosed at least three times, had tricks pull knives on me, have been beaten half to death . . . "

"The abuse and degradation was rough. I sweated and was in deep pain. On top of the horrifying experience, my whole body ached, and I was irritable the whole day. The director didn't really care how I felt; he only wanted to finish the video."[8]

Those are just a few examples of the abuse women in porn endure. So, when someone objects with the claim that women do porn voluntarily, understand that oftentimes the acting required of them is not voluntary; rather, it is harmful. We cannot stay silent about the abuse women are enduring in the porn industry. Only by exposing the realities of the industry will anyone be motivated to speak out against its atrocities. This is one of the reasons I have written this book. People will not fight what they do not know exists.

---

8. Fight the New Drug, "10 Ex-Porn Performers."

3

Porn Hurts Children

IN OCTOBER OF 2019, the #1 most viewed porn video on one of the largest online pornography websites was titled, "My Step-Brother Brazenly Took Advantage of My Helplessness." Laila Mickelwait, President and founder of *New Reality International* and author for *Exodus Cry*, revealed this shocking truth on Twitter. She commented, "in [the video], a young woman gets stuck & her brother rapes her while she says repeatedly "no," "stop," "I'm afraid," & "it hurts."

The sad truth is that this genre of content is not unique at all in the porn industry. In fact, *"incest"* videos were among some of the most searched among porn sites in 2018.[1] Even more disturbing, *"teen"* videos which involve underage teenagers, have also been topping the porn charts for 6 years! Finally, among others, a commonly searched theme is *group sex* scenarios.

> Rape, incest, pedophilia, and group sex. These are some of the most viewed porn videos on the internet today.

An even more disturbing fact is that the Twitter account for the porn website *tried to defend the actors in the video*. They replied to Mickelwait's Twitter thread, arguing that everything that happened

---

1. Fight the New Drug, "Most Viewed Categories."

in the video was 100 percent consensual. While this may be true, it reveals an ugly truth about large porn sites like this and the industry as a whole: they are not concerned about the images of sex being portrayed. They are not standing by, letting users upload their own content. No, the porn industry controls the type of content that is getting people addicted.

What does this mean for young people indulging in pornographic content? They are being fed blatant lies about sex, completely contrary to God's design. But are there negative effects from porn consumption? Aren't these things simply immoral fantasies that we ought not act on? Let us dive into the effects that porn has on the consumer.

A great amount of research has been conducted as to the link between porn consumption and sexual tastes. As was mentioned earlier, one of the leading themes of porn over the past few years has been "teen." Right away, this should raise a major red flag. After all, "teen" is simply an abbreviation for "teenage" which is another word for adolescence. Why is teen porn such a popular theme? Secondly, one can only imagine that many are searching for videos containing younger and younger sexualized subjects.

In many cases, as porn-defenders would argue, the "teens" portrayed in the videos are not actually adolescents. Remember, we have already established that a majority of pornographic content is not real—it is exaggerated, unrealistic acting. To a degree, this is a good thing. But before you get too comfortable with the idea that teenagers are not actually participating in sexually explicit videos, let us take a look at the implications of such content.

Watching videos which even portray the idea of underage people engaging in sexual acts can lead to the desire and curiosity for more extreme scenarios. An article from Fight the New Drug delves into these facts: "Mental health experts have learned that when someone becomes addicted to child porn, they progress to younger and younger children. They seek out more sadistic or masochistic images, and in extreme cases, bestiality."[2] The article goes on.

2. Fight the New Drug, "Mainstream Porn."

Dr. Julie Newberry is a psychologist who has worked with patients who have stories like the one above. In an article for PsychReg[3], she writes: "My therapeutic experience is that a person who views child abuse images, though committing a sexual offense, is not necessarily a pedophile. A pedophile has a primary sexual interest in children. I suggest that for some people, it is porn addiction rather than pedophilia, which is the cause. A person, usually a man, who has no sexual interest in children, can find himself 'crossing the line.'"

She continues on to describe her experience, saying, "[My clients] didn't go onto the internet with the intention of looking at child abuse images, but nevertheless ended up there. They couldn't understand why they continued to do something that disgusted them and which they knew was illegal. I suggest that each of them became desensitized to mild porn and sensitized to extreme porn. Their higher thinking brain, compromised by addiction, could not win the battle, even when it came to viewing child abuse images. Porn sex was too powerful a need and withdrawal too difficult."

The problem is much deeper and more serious than a mere fetish. Porn is ultimately creating a culture of sexual tastes centered around sexual exploitation of teenagers and children. The New York Times published an article in 2019 which explained the remarkable number of images of child sexual abuse floating around the internet.[4] Could this be one of the contributing factors to the pedophilia movement? I say yes, undoubtedly.

It is real, despite the claims that many LGBTQ activists will utter. There is an ongoing movement to normalize pedophilia. In fact, in many instances this is already occurring. Many still recognize the egregiousness of the issue, but many are fighting against the backlash. After all, in a society that has redefined marriage and sexuality completely, why shouldn't pedophilia be wrong?

3. Newberry, "Viewing Child Abuse Images," *Psychreg.*
4. Keller, "The Internet is Overrun," *New York Times.*

PART 1: PORNOGRAPHY

One example is the North American Man-Boy Love Association (NAMBLA). This group is currently attempting to lower the age of consent. What is even more shocking is that, as an ACLU attorney, Justice Ruth Bader once advocated for lowering the age of consent to twelve years old.[5] Nancy Pelosi, the current Speaker of the House, marched with one of the leading activists for "man-boy love" in a 2001 San Francisco gay pride parade.[6] Even more recently, an article on Pink News, a UK-based online newspaper marketed to the lesbian, gay, bisexual and transgender community, featured an article with the headline, "Gay couple Mark, 55, and Kayleb, 22, have been dating for 6 years and regularly get mistaken for father and son." That means they began dating when Kayleb was only 16 years old! I believe the outrageous themes of hardcore pornography are most likely some of the most significant contributors to this terrible movement of sexual culture.

The sad reality, which many are either unaware of or choose to blind themselves to, is that sex trafficking and child sexual abuse are very real and very prevalent in America. The false pornography narratives being spread vicariously throughout the internet are merely fuel for the already raging fire. We as the church have an obligation to step in and act.

5. Whelan, "Slate's Noah on Graham and Ginsburg," *National Review*.
6. Bozell, "Democrats," *Media Research Center*.

4

Porn Affects Our Desires

MANY PRO-PORN ORGANIZATIONS ARE currently pushing the idea that porn is in fact "healthy." These organizations all but ignore the studies that have been conducted and the truths about the harm of the porn industry. In fact, porn is being marketed as something to be celebrated rather than looked down upon. People are more vocal than ever about the benefits of watching pornography (often as opposed to getting involved in real-life sexual relationships). This, of course, is nothing but a blatant lie from the enemy. Satan's sole purpose is to steal, kill, and destroy (John 10:10). In the case of pornography, he seeks to *steal* the purity of young people, *kill* their desires to follow God and his laws, and *destroy* the Biblically ordained concept of marriage and the family. Porn is just one of the many tactics being carried out from the arsenal of Satan, and *it is working*.

The Science of Addiction

When using the term "addiction," the usual imagery which comes to mind is either drugs or alcohol. These are among the most common substances that are abused due to addiction. Other common addictions include shopping, gambling, video games, and *pornography.* All of these can have the same psychological effects on the brain as substance abuse.

Gary Collins says of addictions, "most addictions have no obvious physical cause. Instead, they are behaviors that gain increasing prominence in a person's life and slowly become more and more difficult to control."[1] The word "addiction" is derived from a Latin term for "enslaved by" or "bound to."[2] Addiction occurs when the brain is exposed to a substance, activity, or experience, and over time begins to crave more of it. The satisfaction brought upon by the experience moves from liking to wanting, and finally to *needing*. No one seeks to develop an addiction—it occurs before we are aware. The reason is this: The brain registers all pleasure in the same way. (Get ready for some big words here.) Harvard Health says this:

> In the brain, pleasure has a distinct signature: the release of the neurotransmitter dopamine in the nucleus accumbens, a cluster of nerve cells lying underneath the cerebral cortex. Dopamine release in the nucleus accumbens is so consistently tied with pleasure that neuroscientists refer to the region as the brain's pleasure center. Addictive drugs provide a shortcut to the brain's reward system by flooding the nucleus accumbens with dopamine. The hippocampus lays down memories of this rapid sense of satisfaction, and the amygdala creates a conditioned response to certain stimuli.

In other words, we do not keep returning to something simply because we enjoy it; we return to it because eventually, our brain tells us we have to have it. Certain chemicals in the brain are released, so that only when we experience the thing we are addicted to can the brain's "pleasure center" be satisfied. Until then, all other means fail. The article goes on to say this:

> According to the current theory about addiction, dopamine interacts with another neurotransmitter, glutamate, to take over the brain's system of reward-related learning.

1. Collins, *Christian Counseling*, 688.
2. Harvard Mental Health Letter, "Addiction."

> This system has an important role in sustaining life because it links activities needed for human survival (such as eating and sex) with pleasure and reward ... Repeated exposure to an addictive substance or behavior causes nerve cells in the nucleus accumbens and the prefrontal cortex (the area of the brain involved in planning and executing tasks) to communicate in a way that couples *liking* something with *wanting* it, in turn driving us to go after it. That is, this process motivates us to take action to seek out the source of pleasure.

Addiction not only leads us to desire the substance or activity, it urges us to seek it out. The brain becomes more adapted and "comfortable" with smaller "doses" of the particular substance or activity, and in turn, the desire increases the next time it is exposed. The article continues:

> As a result of these adaptations, dopamine has less impact on the brain's reward center. People who develop an addiction typically find that, in time, the desired substance no longer gives them as much pleasure. They have to take more of it to obtain the same dopamine "high" because their brains have adapted—an effect known as tolerance.

That last sentence is crucial to the issue with pornography. Eventually, addiction leads to stronger desires which are harder to suppress. In addition, the brain requires more and more of the particular experience in order to be satisfied. In the case of porn, *our brains react the same way.* Studies show that pornography produces the exact same psychological reactions as does any other addictive substance. The same principles apply as well—prolonged exposure to pornography becomes more difficult to satisfy.

For example, what may start out as merely viewing images of naked women may develop into watching videos of sexual activity. Sadly, as this habit increases, so does the severity of the content being viewed. The more porn we watch, the harder it is to satisfy the brain. As a result, we move to more hardcore and unrealistic videos to try and please the pleasure center of the brain. In short, the more porn we watch, the more extreme the next video must be. This is

PART 1: PORNOGRAPHY

what has ultimately led to the disturbing categories of sex-videos being consumed daily from major porn providers.

The effects which porn has on one's brain do not stop with an increased desire for hardcore porn, however. Here are some long-term effects of porn consumption *on teenagers* based on a study from ResearchGate:

- Unrealistic sexual beliefs and values
- An over-focus or obsession on sex
- Sexually aggressive behaviors
- Sexually permissive behaviors
- An earlier interest in having sex
- Promiscuity
- Questions about their own body
- Questions about their sexual performance
- Behavior problems
- Depressive feelings
- Bonding issues with others, including their parents[3]

All from watching porn? Absolutely. Do you see the severity of the issue here? Internet porn is not a miniscule issue—and certainly not one that deserves defending. Keep in mind that all of these studies are fairly recent. In light of its rapid growth, there is no way of predicting how far—and how extreme—these effects will become.

Here are a few more examples of research-backed ways in which porn affects sexual desires: Studies have shown that people who watch porn are much more likely to believe that group sex and other dangerous sexual activities are common among the

---

3. Huerta, "Pornography," *Focus on the Family*.

sexually active, and therefore would be more likely to be comfortable engaging in said acts.[4][5][6]

The market which has emerged as a result of excessive porn accessibility creates an increasing demand for the most extreme scenarios of content. Thus, as Dr. John Woods, a therapist who works with adolescents struggling with porn addiction concludes, "This contest to push the boundaries means that straight intercourse is considered too boring. Images of brutal anal sex and women being humiliated and degraded by two or more men at any one time are the new norms."[7]

The Lie

One of the many lies being spread by the porn industry deals with body image. *Porn makes young people question their own bodies.* Porn stars almost always exhibit the physical features that the media consider "sexually desirable." What the market does not tell you is that these standards are exceedingly difficult to achieve—near impossible.

For teenagers and children who are exposed to porn, possibly as their first encounter with sexual activity, they in turn begin to believe the lie that only those features (and behaviors carried out) in the videos are good enough to be considered sexually desirable. This, of course, is another blatant lie. Satan, after all, is the father of lies (John 8:44). He does it best. And sadly, he is coercing people of all ages into this false narrative.

As a result, many young people experience depression as a result of porn exposure—they feel they will never be able to measure up the standards they see in porn. More heartbreaking, as we discussed earlier, many sexual partners who are addicted to porn begin to expect the same type of sexual experience as he or she

---

4. Weinberg et al., "Pornography," *Archives of Sexual Behavior,* 39 (6) 1389–1401.

5. Layden, Pornography Addiction.

6. Zillmann, "Influence," *Journal of Adolescent Health,* 27(2), 41–44.

7. Woods, "Jamie is 13," *Daily Mail UK.*.

sees in porn-shoots. Consequently, the porn-viewer's partner cannot match the expectations. And thus, the sex-life, the most sacred aspect of a Godly marriage, is torn apart.

For others, the opposite effect is true—they buy into the false narrative that the human body is nothing more than an object of sexual pleasure. Thus, we see many teenagers dressing provocatively and becoming more and more comfortable posing for social media in such senses (see chapter 9). Once the lie is sold that we are nothing more than the sum of all the sexual pleasure our bodies can provide, the meaning and value of life and of the spirit have been deprived of us. We are left as nothing more than physical beings. Ironically, this is the conclusion that naturally follows from a naturalistic, atheistic, and nihilistic worldview. This is the exact narrative that porn is producing: sex is just that. It is nothing more than a transactional encounter between two (or more) human beings. *Time* magazine reported, "Many [young boys] are simply unable to experience a sexual response with a real live woman."[8] What a tragic consequence.

The effects are not temporary either; they are long-term, potentially tearing marriages apart. Nancy Pearcy writes, "The first longitudinal study on porn found that men who start watching porn after they marry are twice as likely to divorce. Other studies found that watching porn actually shrinks the brain and reduces neural activity."[9]

Gary Brooks, a psychology professor who studies the effects of pornography, says, "It's sad. Boys who are initiated in [to] sex through these images become indoctrinated in a way that can potentially stay with them for the rest of their lives."[10] *Indoctrination*. This is what is occurring through the porn industry. But do not let that title fool you: who is the real enemy here? Satan. He is tearing apart the boundaries of marriage and sex put in place by the Creator of marriage himself, and replacing them with a perverted, distorted lie. There is something much deeper at play

---

8. Luscombe, "Porn," *Time*.
9. Pearcey, *Love Thy Body*, 126.
10. Paul, *Pornified*, 187.

than simple immoral imagery on a screen. Porn is a spiritual issue, and a portal to demonic activity.

Porn Is a Spiritual Issue

"For our struggle is not against flesh and blood, but against the rulers, against the powers, against the world forces of this darkness, against the spiritual forces of wickedness in the heavenly places" (Ephesians 6:12). As real as is the physical world of pornography, there are deeper forces at play behind the scenes as well. Do not let the stark reality of the horrors of porn distract you from the true nature of sinful activity.

One of the most overlooked themes in all the Bible is demonic activity. Unfortunately, it is very real and very alive in the world as we know it. David Jeremiah describes the spiritual realm this way: "Spirits are invisible, but their activities are evident." Very evident at that. Do not be ignorant of the strategies being carried out by Satan and his fallen angels. They are at play within the porn industry. Scripture speaks on the topic of sexual immorality, and it is always severely negative. It is the sin Paul describes as being unique to any other sin, in that we are sinning against our own bodies, as opposed to sinning outside the body (1 Corinthians 6:18).

Pornography is a powerful tactic that can be used by Satan to allow demonic activity into our lives. Understand the reality of this truth; it is a parasite that is eating away at people, even children. We as followers of Christ must be willing to stand against the demonic forces and prevent demonic activity from taking captive the hearts and minds of children and teenagers.

5

The Prevalence of Pornography

Just How Easy Is it to Watch Porn?

LONG AGO ARE THE days during which it was difficult to access pornography. As we have already discussed, pornographic content used to be reserved to specific retailers, available only to those who were of age and were willing to approach the counter to ask for a magazine or video. Now, anyone with a computer or mobile device of any kind can access porn in a matter of seconds. Unless specific search filters have been applied to an internet browser, one simple keyword will unlock seemingly endless archives of pornographic pictures and videos. So, any device that has internet access can potentially be used to view pornography.

In fact, many porn websites have ceased asking the question "Are you at least 18 years of age?" before allowing access to the website (not that such a question would have stopped many underage viewers to begin with.) Even so, this demonstrates the industry's apathy toward child-exposure to pornography, and thus explains the alarming ages at which children are seeing porn for the first time. The American Academy of Pediatrics reported that of children between the ages of 10 and 17 years old, 42 percent of them have watched pornography online.[1]

What is even more sad is that even non-pornographic websites often feature pornographic content. Tublr, the popular "microblogging" site, was recently under fire and had to change some of the guidelines because of an increase of adult content, referred to by users as "NSFW" (Not Safe for Work). Tublr hosts more than 23 million active users; According to Pew Research, 23 percent of teen girls use the platform, compared to a mere 5 percent of boys. The website does allow said adult content, and actually requests that its users tag the content as "adult" before posting it, though there is no guarantee these guidelines will always be followed.

Popular websites such as iFunny have also been reported to feature pornographic content. These platforms exist freely for users to upload shared content. There are algorithms in place for catching explicit content and prohibiting it, but these systems do not always prove accurate. Some adult content always seems to slip through the filter. In fact, many users have caught onto this and have created accounts dedicated to sneaking pornography onto the website. They do so by uploading videos consisting of about 20 seconds of random, clean content which then switches to completely exposed porn clips for the remainder of the video. This way, the moderators of iFunny will be fooled into thinking the videos are harmless, though very explicit content is lurking toward the end.

The major porn providers proudly host accounts on platforms like Instagram and Twitter as well. Though they do not actually post any of their content on the social media pages, it is as easy to follow them as tapping on their account pages. From there, viewers are then exposed to all sorts of advertising posted to the pages, and even "trailers" to the latest porn videos!

This wide-spread availability of pornographic content must come to a stop. Through it all, we must be aware of the dangers of pornography and the prevalent nature of this tactic of temptation from the Enemy.

---

1. Hennessy et al., "Estimating," *Journal of Sex Research*, 586–596.

PART 1: PORNOGRAPHY

Answering Objections to Porn-Supporters

Why should we limit an individual's right to watch porn? Alcohol and smoking also have detrimental effects, but those things are legal, right?

This is not a matter of trying to take away someone's right, it is a matter of protecting the psychological health of people—especially children! Besides, no one has the "right" to watch porn. People have the right to upload content to the internet, but that does not mean the content is morally good. If a substance or behavior is harmful to both the consumers and the society, I believe it deserves to be spoken out against.

Secondly, the difference between porn and, say, alcohol abuse, is small. That much is true. Both can lead to addiction, both can lead to behavioral changes (even though the behavioral changes for porn-addicts is much more long-term), and both are immoral.[2] However, the difference is this: alcohol in and of itself is not immoral; how it is used, or *abused* is what leads to immorality. On the contrary, pornography is always immoral, because it satisfies lustful desires wrongly. From a Biblical standpoint, this is wrong. The words of Jesus were: "but I say to you that everyone who looks at a woman with lust for her has already committed adultery with her in his heart." (Matthew 5:28). Also, remember why there was a prohibition movement—one of the driving reasons was to decrease spousal abuse. Just like with alcohol, porn can lead to abusive (sexual) behavior, which in turn can destroy relationships and the potential thereof.

---

2. The topic of alcohol consumption is another point that needs addressing, though this is not the book for that conversation. For clarity, however, here is my basic position on alcohol: drinking alcohol is not wrong, but drunkenness is (Galatians 5:21, Ephesians 5:18). We are called to be sober-minded (1 Peter 5:8–9). This principle applies to things like smoking marijuana as well—the issue is not with the thing itself, but with how it is used, *or abused*. Even Jesus drank alcohol (this is evidenced by the people's accusations of him being a "drunkard" (Luke 7:33–44)). Of course, Jesus never got drunk, being that he lived a sinless life and drunkenness is clearly condemned as sin.

THE PREVALENCE OF PORNOGRAPHY

Okay, maybe hardcore porn is bad, but what about softcore porn?

Again, the issue is not so much with the fact that porn exists; it is the fact that so many people are being exposed to it at young ages and getting addicted. Besides, regardless of the degree of severity acted out in porn videos, I discussed earlier how prolonged exposure to pornographic content only creates a need for more extreme content. So-called "softcore" porn may seem harmless but will ultimately lead to hardcore porn consumption.

You might think it is wrong but stop imposing your morality on me!

Why, would it be *immoral* for me to "impose my morality?" That is a self-defeating objection. Author and apologist, Frank Turek, when faced with this objection to a particular issue, says "this is not *my* morality. I did not make this stuff up." In other words, it is not *my* morality to say that murder, rape, theft, and pedophilia are wrong. I did not decide the men were made for women and women for men, and the best way to perpetuate and stabilize society is to preserve that structure of marriage.[3] And I did not decide that pornography is wrong (much less, harmful!) So, to say that I am imposing my morality by speaking out against porn consumption and the porn industry is a false conclusion.

What about "feminist porn?"

Feminist porn is pornography in which the female in the video dominates the sexual encounter. This is an often-used objection against anti-porn arguments because it suggests that feminist porn is at least a safe alternative for the actresses, being that they are not harmed and objectified in the videos.

The problem with this argument is that it still undermines the effects porn has on the consumers. Even though they may be right in saying it is "better" because at least less females are being harmed,

---

3. For an in-depth argument on the topic of same-sex marriage, read *Correct, Not Politically Correct: How Same-Sex Marriage Hurts Everyone* by Frank Turek.

that does not negate the harmfulness of porn as-a-whole. Besides, there is no way of knowing simply from a viewer-standpoint which videos are harmful to any of the actors/actresses involved.

6

What Can I Do?

How to Safeguard Your Devices

HERE ARE SOME VERY practical ways to block pornographic content from your computer or your child's computer/phone. Although it is almost impossible to completely eradicate a device from any access to adult content, because of its prevalence on the internet, these tips and tricks will make it much more difficult to accidentally or intentionally come across porn. Also, I have included monitoring methods such as disabling private browsing modes so that it will be easier to be aware of what is being viewed on a particular device.

Activate Google SafeSearch

1. Go to Search Settings.
2. Find the "SafeSearch filters" section. To turn on SafeSearch, check the box next to "Filter explicit results."
3. At the bottom of the screen, tap Save.

PART 1: PORNOGRAPHY

Limit Adult Content and Disable Private Browsing

For iPhone/iPad

Private browsing is a method of browsing the internet that does not save any history, cookies, or cache. In other words, browsing in private mode (Incognito Mode for Google Chrome) does not leave a trace. Luckily, there is a way to disable private browsing on Apple Devices.

1. Open the "Settings" app in iOS.
2. Go to "General" and then to "Screen Time" then choose the "Restrictions" option (older iOS versions go directly from General > Restrictions)
3. Choose to Enable Restrictions and enter a passcode. This is a good opportunity to set a personal passcode that only you know, so that your child cannot access these settings without your permission.
4. scroll down to find "Websites" and choose "Limit Adult Content" to enable a web filter in Safari; this will *completely disable Private Browsing mode in Safari for iOS* and it completely removes the Private button in Safari tabs.

Now, the device should be free of adult content as well as private browsing *in safari*. Additionally, should you decide to download a third-party browser as a separate app, the adult content filter will still be applied, and pornographic content will be restricted. This setting also removes the option to delete browsing history through Safari.

WHAT CAN I DO?

How to Disable Incognito Mode (Google Chrome)

For Windows

Method 1:

1. Select *"Start"* and type *"CMD"* into the search box.
2. Right-click *Command Prompt* and select *Run as Administrator*.
3. In the Command Prompt window, type REG ADD HKLM\SOFTWARE\Policies\Google\Chrome /v IncognitoModeAvailability /t REG_DWORD /d 1, then press Enter. [/NL 1–3]

Method 2:

1. Hold down the *Windows Key* and press *"R"* to bring up the Run box.
2. Type *"regedit,"* then press *"Enter."*
3. Navigate to *"HKEY_LOCAL_MACHINE"* > *"SOFTWARE"* > *"Policies"* > *"Google"* > *"Chrome."*
4. *Note: You may have to create the* "Google" *and* "Chrome" *folders.*
5. Right-click *"Chrome"* and select *"New"* > *"DWORD 32-bit value"*
6. Give the value a name of *"IncognitoModeAvailability."*
7. Double-click on *"IncognitoModeAvailability."* A box will appear where you can set the value data to *"1."*
8. Restart the computer, and the option to select *"Incognito Mode"* in Google Chrome will be gone.

For Mac

1. In the Finder, click *"Go"* > Utilities.

2. Open the Terminal app.
3. Type "defaults write com.google.chrome IncognitoModeAvailability -integer 1z" and then press *Enter*.

Use Content Filters

I have not analyzed all content filters that are available, but there are many out there. For instance, one that is very useful and user-friendly is "**BlockSite**" for Google Chrome. It is a free add-on for the Chrome browser, and allows you to block specific websites, keywords, and adult content. You can have it set to block any website with the word "porn" or any other explicit, sexual phrases in the URL. Additionally, you can set a password so that these settings cannot be changed until the password is entered. You can also set it to redirect the user to a different website of choice whenever blocked websites are searched.

Other filters include:

- Net Nanny
- Covenant Eyes
- Forcefield
- Bsecure Online
- rTribe

Fighting Back

Like all sin, porn is not permanently enslaving. Christ rescues us from our bondage to sin. Thanks to his sacrifice on the cross, we can find redemption and forgiveness. God's grace covers our sin, and with it we have hope and comfort.

If you or your children are currently on the front lines of the war with pornography, *you are not alone*. It can feel like a lonely (and often hopeless) battle. Remember that there is help available.

Seek Christian counseling and accountability. Remember that this is an urgent matter; do not wait to take action.

There is a helpful article from Danny Huerta of Focus on the Family dealing with helping teenagers combat the temptation of pornography. I will simply address the main points.

1. **Teach your teen how to manage stress.** Viewing porn is often an outlet for stress-relief for many teenagers. Unfortunately, it is also an outlet for escaping loneliness. Huerta makes these points: As a parent, ask yourself how you are modeling stress management. Do you have good self-care relative to balancing relationships, renewal, and work? Do you leave enough margin in your life for some down time? Do you spend time with your Heavenly Father? (Isaiah 26:3-4, Psalm 56:3).

2. **Place limits on technology.** Huerta writes, "Homes need to have limits for computer time, video games, television, movies, music and phones . . . Some things to consider: Technology opens the door to a wide, wide world and some kids can manage that freedom. Others can't. There's no rush. They grow up fast enough. Make decisions based on what's best for your family, not what the neighbors are doing."

3. **Create an open device policy.** Clearly outline which websites are allowed. Huerta suggests outlining sites your children are allowed to visit, times of day they can access the Web, length of time they're allowed to be online, appropriate consequences for breaking the rules (i.e., losing phone privilege,) and privileges for following the rules (i.e., extended time with friends or other increased freedoms)

4. **Teach the difference between wants and needs.** This is where a Biblical foundation is vital. We must understand the importance of God's law as laid out in Scripture, and why our sexual desires lead to sin if not within the context which God laid out in his Word. Pornography is a want, but it will never satisfy. It always leaves us wanting more.

5. **Talk about sex, oxytocin, and mindset.** We have already addressed the facts about porn and its direct link to addiction. Discussing these effects, Huerta describes the different areas of our lives that porn can take captive. "Sexual desire (Pornography consumes it). Sexual arousal (Pornography distorts it). Sexual behaviors (Pornography controls it). Sexual functioning (Pornography creates dysfunction.)"

6. **Help your teen cultivate wise risk-taking and decision-making.** "Pornography can be an exciting risk, because it can create novelty, excitement and an illusion of feeling grown up or pursued."

7. **Encourage a close and authentic relationship with God, you, and others.** Strong relationships are probably the most important practical step toward freedom from the bonds of porn.[1]

What is the Solution?

Pornography is a sin; that much is clear. The consequences and after-effects do differ, however. Even so, the Bible offers grace to sinners no matter which sin he or she is battling. Though all sin is not the same, all sin requires the same punishment—the wrath of God, which is manifested in an eternity in hell. However, God in his grace offers a way to redemption: the perfect sacrifice of his son, Jesus Christ.

While sin is deserving of the same punishment, there is no promise that we will not reap the consequences of our sin while on earth, either. However, there is a promise that we can have eternal life if we choose to acknowledge our sin and turn to Jesus. As Scripture says, if we confess with our mouths that Jesus is Lord and believe that God raised him from the dead, we will be saved (Romans 10:9–10). Also, *everyone* who calls on the name of the Lord will be saved (Romans 10:13). The solution is nothing we can

---

1. Huerta, "Strategies," *Focus on the Family.*

do, but everything that Christ has already done—his atoning work on the cross as an outpouring of his abundant love for us covers our all sin, so that everyone can be rescued from the bondage of pornography addiction. You are not alone in this fight. There is always hope because Jesus made a way.

So, the eternal solution to every sin is Christ. He is the only way we can be freed of our slavery to sin. If you are allowing your addiction to pornography to define you, or you have a child who is doing the same, remember that the only remedy to being defined by sin is allowing our Creator to define us. We are made in God's image (Genesis 1:27). And once we allow his grace to cover our sins, he calls us sons and daughters and adopts us into a new family—the family of God. And one day we will be able to rest eternally with him in his kingdom if we choose to put our trust in him.

Don't Lose Hope

I hope that this has opened your eyes to some of the truths about pornography and the porn industry if you were not already aware. It is important, though, that we do not lose hope. Yes, it seems like Satan has a tight grasp on our sexualized society. But remember, God is sovereign (Job 42:2, Psalm 135:6, Proverbs 19:21, 1 Chronicles 9:11–12). He is above all things and is in control of all things. If we stay faithful to him, we can combat the temptation of pornography.

What does all of this mean for the parent or guardian? *Stay faithful to the Word.* The days are evil (Ephesians 5:16), and Satan is prowling around like a roaring lion, looking to entice people with the lies of porn. So, guard your hearts and minds (Philippians 4:7) and train up your children in the way they should go. Then they will not depart from it (Proverbs 22:6). Remember that this is a battle we all must face together as the body of Christ.

Part 2: **Media**

7

Liars

FROM THE BEGINNING OF time, the number 1 tactic of the enemy has been the same. *Lies.* As far back as the Garden of Eden, before sin had ever entered the world and God cursed the earth, lies have been the most prominent weapon of Satan. "Did God actually say . . .?"

The account is laid out in Genesis chapter 3, in which humanity falls into depravity from God. It is this story which sets the stage for the rest of Scripture; the need for a Savior is Genesis 3, the reason for evil is Genesis 3, the reason why there is disease, sorrow, and death—all of this stems from Genesis 3. And the one decision that plunged humanity into its fallen state was after a lie from Satan. It was a lie that sought to refute everything God had commanded Adam and Eve. It sought to undermine the authority of God's promises. God assured Adam and Eve that they would die upon consumption of the forbidden fruit from the tree of the knowledge of good and evil. Satan convinced them this was not true.

> Now the serpent was more crafty than any beast of the field which the Lord God had made. And he said to the woman, "Indeed, has God said, 'You shall not eat from any tree of the garden'?" The woman said to the serpent, "From the fruit of the trees of the garden we may eat; but from the fruit of the tree which is in the middle of the

> garden, God has said, 'You shall not eat from it or touch it, or you will die.'" The serpent said to the woman, "You surely will not die! For God knows that in the day you eat from it your eyes will be opened, and you will be like God, knowing good and evil."

Satan is a liar, and God is truth. When we believe the lies of Satan over the truth of God, there will always be disastrous consequences. Unfortunately, these tactics are still all too real today. And children are often the targets of these attacks, which is exactly why parents must be willing to defend against them with the truth of Scripture. In fact, Jesus makes a strong case about the importance of children being deceived, even by us! In Matthew 18:6, he says, "but whoever causes one of these little ones who believe in Me to stumble, it would be better for him to have a heavy millstone hung around his neck, and to be drowned in the depth of the sea." That seems a bit extreme, don't you think, Jesus?

Jesus was tough. He spoke the truth. And sometimes, truth is not easy to hear. From this verse, we observe the severity of leading children away from truth—yet this is exactly what Satan seeks to do. And his arsenal gets updated with every new technological advancement that is unveiled. One example of this is the world of internet media. We have already exposed the truth about pornography; now I want to delve into the dangers of media exposure in general, focusing on popular outlets such as social media. Are they dangerous?

Before we get to exposing *lies*, though, we must have a firm grasp on *truth*.

What Is Truth?

> Therefore Pilate entered again into the Praetorium, and summoned Jesus and said to Him, "Are You the King of the Jews?" Jesus answered, "Are you saying this on your own initiative, or did others tell you about Me?" Pilate answered, "I am not a Jew, am I? Your own nation and the chief priests delivered You to me; what have You done?"

> Jesus answered, "My kingdom is not of this world. If My kingdom were of this world, then My servants would be fighting so that I would not be handed over to the Jews; but as it is, My kingdom is not of this realm." Therefore Pilate said to Him, "So You are a king?" Jesus answered, "You say correctly that I am a king. For this I have been born, and for this I have come into the world, to testify to the truth. Everyone who is of the truth hears My voice." Pilate said to Him, "What is truth?"

Certainly, this is not a difficult question to answer, right? Unfortunately, in a culture that has abandoned it, a simple definition is not as easy to recognize. For our intents and purposes, I will briefly address the topic. Truth is that which affirms reality for what it really is. In other words, truth corresponds to and matches its object. This is what is known as *absolutism*. For truth to be absolute, it cannot change depending on one's perspective of a particular topic. That is the opposite approach to truth, which many try to argue for, known as *relativism*. Relativists believe that all truth is just that—relative. In other words, truth is whatever you want it to be. You can probably already start to see the detrimental implications of relativism.

Absolute truth can be defended by three laws: the law of noncontradiction, the law of excluded middle, and the law of identity. The law of noncontradiction says that no two opposing claims can both be true at the same time and in the same sense. For example, God cannot both exist (the theistic worldview) and not exist (the atheistic worldview) at the same time. One of these claims is absolutely true, and the opposite (as well as every other claim which opposes it) must be absolutely false. The law of excluded middle says that a claim is either absolutely true or absolutely false, with no middle ground. Going back to our example of God's existence, God either absolutely does exist at all times in all places for every person, or he does not exist at all. There is no in-between. God cannot exist for some and not for others; he cannot exist only at certain times of the year and not during the rest of time. No, if God exists, then he exists absolutely and with no exceptions. This brings us to the final law—the law of identity. This law says that if something is true, then it is true. That is the "identity" of the claim. Once again, using our example, if God exists, then he exists. Period. Choosing not to believe in God does not make him go away.

Whew. That was a lot of information, I know, but I believe it is important to have a proper grasp on the nature of truth in order to combat the lies of relativism being spread throughout the culture. Children need a foundation of absolute truth in order to build their worldview on a source that will not crumble at the expense of the Enemy's schemes. This source of truth can be none other than God's Word—the most reliable and trustworthy source of truth.

Now that we know what truth *is,* we can rightfully discern what it *is not.* Truth is not relative. Truth is not simply what makes us feel good. Truth is not what the majority says, and it is not what is believed. "Jesus said to him, "I am the way, and the truth, and the life; no one comes to the Father but through Me.""" (John 14:6). Discipleship begins in the home, and this is why a coherent understanding of truth is so vital to children. They need to know that God is love and *truth.*

8

Music

IF THERE IS ONE thing that can unite a group of people, it is sharing a favorite music group or artist. With the rise of so many artists, which seem to be popping up every five minutes, it is almost impossible to keep up with the mainstream music industry. Like pornography, music is much more easily accessible than ever. At one time, only a few decades ago, music was only available either on the radio or to be bought from the music store.

There is a common joke among people who grew up in the earlier eras of music that children do not have any idea what a cassette tape is. Luckily, vinyl records have come back in style, which I find very cool. Even so, music can now be streamed online, which is the most common way to listen. Streaming services like Spotify, Apple Music, and Pandora provide listeners with literally endless access to practically every artist who has ever recorded music. That being said, just what are the kids listening to these days?

I want to give you just an example of some of the lyrics from some of the most streamed artists among children and teenagers within the past few years.

One of the most streamed and downloaded artists of 2018, known as "Tekashi 6ix9ine," has a song titled, "Billy," with lyrics that were so explicit, I cannot write them out in this book. Essentially, there are lines in the song which are as descriptively graphic as are some porn videos. Another widely popular fresh-on-the scene artist, with more than four million listeners on Spotify, has one song that repeats a line about waking up, throwing up, and feeling like he is dead throughout the chorus of the song. Granted, these artists are not typically heard on major radio stations for that very reason. However, some of the most listened to songs of the past few years which are available on the radio's pop stations are just as bad.

The entire song, *Cake by the Ocean* by DNCE and Nick Jonas is about sex and describes it with sexually metaphoric language. This song topped the charts in the summer of 2018. The song *Locked Out of Heaven* by Bruno Mars is playing on the idea of heaven but is describing a sexual relationship that prevents Bruno from being able to enter heaven. The sex, according to Bruno, is better than heaven, though. Bruno Mars is one of the most streamed artists as well.

One of the most recent artists on the scene, a girl named Billie Eilish, has some particularly disturbing lyrics. Even so, she is currently the 8th most streamed artist on Spotify, with more than 50 million monthly listeners! She has a song titled *all the good girls go to hell,* and due to copyrights, I cannot quote the lyrics directly. However, they describe good girls going to hell, as the strange title implies, along with God, referred to as a woman, having enemies. This is followed by Eilish stating that the good girl will want Satan to be on her team, and that her Lucifer is lonely. She concludes this section of the song claiming that God will owe her for something. Overall, it is an unsettling vibe; did I mention that *this girl was 17 years old* when she wrote the song?

There is even a song that is literally titled *Date Rape,* by a band called Sublime. The song is about exactly what the title suggests and goes into more detail than you would want. Again, due to copyrights, I cannot quote the lyrics directly, though it is probably better that I refrain anyways. The pre-chorus and chorus describe the girl not wanting to do anything sexual, but the singer admits that if not for date rape, he would not have had sex with her. The sexualized lyrics alone in music is mind-blowing. What is strange is that these songs become "trendy," and make their way into popular video tends, such as with apps like TikTok, and thus children and teenagers become accustomed to the sexually saturated lyrics. If you don't believe me, there are playlists of trending TikTok songs which are updated regularly on music outlets such as Spotify. Take a listen; only a few songs will give you a glimpse into the most popular music among children and teenagers today.

I could go on and on and keep listing the disturbing lyrics of popular music, from songs praising suicide[1] to songs praising murder, to a very recent song by two female hip-hop artists that topped the charts, which describes the degradation and prostitution of women in detail as something to be praised. Obviously, there is a serious threat within the music industry. And of course, I am not for a second suggesting that there has never been explicit music until now. No, but what I am saying is that children and teenagers are being exposed to these songs, possibly without even realizing what they are about! The sad truth, as you might expect, is that the "Parental Advisory: Explicit Content" warning that is posted on the cover of albums featuring explicit lyrics is rarely followed. It is probably not even noticed anymore, considering how commonly it is seen.

Album covers themselves are even becoming less filtered. One example is a very popular artist known as Cardi B; one of her albums features an image of her drinking from a bottle of what is obviously alcohol, while a man can be clearly seen to be engaging in oral sex with her. Though nothing is actually uncovered in the picture, it is obvious what is going on.

We must realize the implications of what is happening here. These are the artists who are potentially influencing young

---

1. There is a song that was popular when I was in middle school, but that many teenagers and children are aware of today and can probably recite the lyrics to. It is called *Welcome to the Black Parade* by My Chemical Romance. The song is essentially about suicide. The band is a genre called "emo" (short for *emotional*) which exhibits a lot of disturbingly dark lyrics. Another example is the song *Last Resort* by Papa Roach, which also discusses suicide rather graphically. I will not list the lyrics here, but feel free to look them up or take a listen to hear for yourself.

people. I am not suggesting that secular music is all bad and that we should only listen to so-called "Christian music"[2] by any means, but I do believe that all the music we listen to, especially as Christians, should be honoring to God. As Paul says, "So, whether you eat or drink, or whatever you do, do all to the glory of God" (1 Corinthians 10:31).

Okay, But Isn't It Just Music?

So what? Why should we care if young people are listening to music that glorifies things that Christians consider immoral?

Though there is still much research to be done as to the correlation between music and behavior, many studies are currently being conducted. One study concluded that there is in fact a relationship between certain music genres and antisocial behavior, vulnerability to suicide, and drug use.[3] Whether or not the music is the *cause* of, or even a contributing factor to these behaviors is yet to be determined; however, the behaviors listed are negative. According to many studies, the portrayal of violence in a positive light has only increased over the years, and as a result become more prevalent in music as well. This is often associated with the wealth, success, and masculinity of the artists. So, there is a potential for a correlation between lyrics and behaviors, though an exact conclusion is vague at this point. Also, music is influential. Lyrics have power; sexualized lyrics will often lead to curiosity, which in turn can lead to internet searches which are destined to result in pornography.

However, this is not a Christian stance, though my motivations for addressing it are certainly rooted in my Christian worldview. This is a moral stance. Any music that glorifies rape, violence, and suicide should not be praised or available for public streaming, especially since children and teenagers are the ones who are being influenced

---

2. I use quotations because there is no such thing as "Christian" music. Music cannot be Christian any more than a chair can be Christian. Music can be *made* by Christians and used to glorify God, but music itself is not "Christian."

3. Baker and Bor, "Music Preference," *Sage Journals.*

MUSIC

the most. Secondly, music promotes culture. Music is one of many traits that help define a culture, and if a culture of young people is united by music that glorifies immoral acts, this is a detriment to a rightly-functioning and morally astute society.

Luckily, most music streaming services offer the option to restrict access to explicit content.

For Spotify

Mobile

1. Tap Home.
2. Tap Settings.
3. Tap *Explicit Content*.
4. Switch Allow *Explicit Content* off (gray).
5. Tracks marked as *explicit* now appear grayed out. It's not possible to play them and they are skipped over by the player.[4]

Desktop

1. Click the arrow in the top-right corner and select *Settings*.
2. Under *Explicit Content*, switch *Allow playback of explicit-rated content* off (gray).

For Pandora

Set the Explicit Filter from Mobile Device

1. Tap the *Profile* icon, followed by the *Settings* gear in the top right corner.
2. Select *Account*.

4. This information was taken from support.spotify.com.

3. To *filter* explicit content, switch the *Allow Explicit Content* option to *Off* (grey). To *allow* explicit content, switch the *Allow Explicit Content* option to *On* (green).

4. Tap *Save*, then enter your password to confirm the changes.

Set the Explicit Filter from Computer

1. Click the icon (initial or picture) in the top right corner then select *Settings > Content Settings*.

2. Toggle the Explicit Content setting to "Off" to block explicit content (the switch will appear grey). Setting it to "On" will allow explicit content (the switch will be green).

3. Click the *Save Changes* button when finished and enter your password to confirm the changes.

Filtering Explicit Content from Podcasts

Pandora's explicit content filter only applies to stations, not podcasts. However, you can identify explicit episodes by the red "*E*" label.

Filtering Explicit Content on Pandora Premium

As with podcasts, Pandora's explicit content filter doesn't apply to playlists you create, or those created for you by Pandora. You can identify explicit tracks by a red "*E*" label. To keep explicit songs from your playlists, avoid adding songs with this label.

MUSIC

If Pandora creates a playlist for you with an explicit track you'd like to remove, copy that playlist into a new playlist, and then remove any explicit tracks.[5]

For Apple Music

Go to Settings > General > Restrictions > Enable Restrictions and set a passcode > Scroll down to Allowed Content > Music, News & iTunes U and turn off the Explicit toggle switch.

---

5. This information was taken from help.pandora.com.

9

Social Media

ACCORDING TO AMANDA LENHART of Pew Research Center, "Aided by the convenience and constant access provided by mobile devices, especially smartphones, 92% of teens report going online daily—including 24% who say they go online "almost constantly."[1] We have already briefly discussed the dangers of explicit content on social media, looking specifically at Tumblr. Let us take a look at some of the other most popular social media platforms being used by young people today and evaluate the potential threats which lurk there.

Snapchat

I thought the concept was ridiculous when I first learned about it; Snapchat came onto the social media scene in 2011. It allowed users to take and send pictures to other people they follow—however, the pictures were only available for a few seconds, after which they can never be seen again. Now, more features have been added to the app. Users can now send videos and pictures with captions written on them. Snapchat was also the first to introduce the "story" feature, which is essentially a highlight that is posted by

---

1. Lenhart, "Teens," *Pew Research Center.*

the user and only available for 24 hours but can be viewed as many times as desired. Now, Instagram and Facebook also have stories. Snapchat is widely popular among teenagers, with 40 percent of teens ages 13 to 17 actively using the app as of 2015.

The concerning aspect of Snapchat is the one thing that makes it unique. Images and videos which are sent through the app are only seen one time. (Users can, however, choose to "replay" a snap, which provides them the chance to view the image or video a second time.) After that, the picture or video can never be seen again.

The app became very popular among teenagers and young people almost instantly. However, it also became a great way for people to send explicit photos of themselves (known as "sexting") with virtually no consequence. After all, the photos no longer exist after they have been viewed. Even today, Snapchat is often used to send certain photos to certain people, which users want to keep secret. The danger of this is two-fold: first, the idea of photos that disappear obviously has plenty of negative implications. There is virtually no way of knowing what Snapchat users are sending or receiving via the app. Secondly, all phones have the ability to take a screenshot. This captures whatever is on the screen of the phone as a separate image. Many devices also feature screen-recording, which allows users to capture the activity of their device in the form of a video.

The danger of this is that, as you may have already guessed, Snapchat photos potentially never disappear, if the recipient of the photo chooses to screenshot the snap. The app does notify the sender when this happens, but there is also the option of using a third-party photo capturing app or software, which does not notify the sender. So, while sending explicit photos to friends or significant others should not be occurring anyways, there is an additional risk involved of not knowing whether the recipient has decided to keep the photo/video, and with whom he or she could potentially share it. Please be aware of what your child is sending/receiving via Snapchat, and who they relate to on the app.

Snapchat also contains a "discover" section, where users can view and follow worldwide content posted by popular user accounts

PART 2: MEDIA

across the globe. These include content accounts such as BuzzFeed, Cosmopolitan, Vice, and various celebrities who may also have Snapchat. In 2016, however, a lawsuit was filed in California which cited some sexual content that was available in the Discover section. Some examples of said content included stories such as "people share their secret rules for sex," "10 things he thinks when he can't make you orgasm," and a BuzzFeed feature titled, "23 Pictures That Are Too Real If You've Ever Had Sex With A Penis."[2]

Lastly, Snapchat offers users the option of being active on "Snap Map," which visually shows where all users who have the feature active are located at any given point. For example, if I have Snap Map active, my account (displayed by a cartoon version of me which I customize) will tell other users where I am. If I am in Walt Disney World, my followers know it. If I am at my house, they know that as well. The danger of any social media, as I will address more thoroughly later in this chapter, is connecting with "friends" who may not be real friends after all. They may be predators, stalkers, etc. who now have direct access to one's location.

Facebook/Instagram

"Facebook remains the most used social media site among American teens ages 13 to 17 with 71% of all teens using the site, even as half of teens use Instagram and four-in-ten use Snapchat," Lenhart says. 71 percent of all teenagers; that is a big number! The threats facing users of these social media platforms are similar to those which have already been addressed regarding Snapchat. In fact, many social media platforms have begun to adapt many of the same features as those of their main competitors. For example, most of the major platforms allow photo/video posting, direct messaging through chat, photo, or video, live video streaming, and the ability to like, comment, and share content. Facebook is possibly the

2. Read the entire document online here: https://www.scribd.com/document/317728807/Snapchat-Indecency-Lawsuit#from_embed?campaign=SkimbitLtd&ad_group=66960X1514734X01af3ea8857dbafef54370182bad14ba&keyword=660149026&source=hp_affiliate&medium=affiliate

most syncretistic, offering users a marketplace for selling to other friends, and even a dating feature!

The culture created by social media, however, is what harms young people. As was mentioned earlier, social media, like internet porn, is a fairly recent invention. While social media in and of itself has been around since 1979, following the creation of a platform known as "Usenet," social media as a popular form of networking did not take off until Facebook in 2006. That makes for less than two decades during which social media use has been prevalent in American society! Now it seems that practically every American is active on at least one form of social media, regardless of which generation they belong to.

The narrative being sold by social media is not necessarily a creation of the outlets themselves. It is a product of the rapid growth of social media, and the desire to be "noticed" on the internet. To which narrative am I referring? Many refer to it as the "selfie-generation"; it is the ego-centric complex that arises in many social media users. One statistic concluded that people took a collective 93 *million* "selfies" (photos of themselves, taken by themselves) every day in 2014.[3] So, what is the danger of posting pictures of oneself?

While posting a picture of yourself on social media is not the issue in and of itself, the culture created by excessive social media involvement is dangerous. Social media provides users with an outlet to share as much or as little of their lives as they choose. The natural result of this is, of course, that only the highlights are posted. No one wants to share the low points of his or her life for every follower to see. So, we post only the pictures of ourselves that were taken at just the right angle, with just the right lighting, exposing only our "good side," and with the best-looking face we can make for the camera. Do not be fooled, this is exactly what the mainstream media does for models on the covers of magazines. There are no one-and-done photo shoots. Many shoots take several hours just to get a few good shots. A lot of what is displayed on magazine and website fronts are even

---

3. Brandt, "Google divulges," *Silicon Valley Business Journal.*

edited by photo-editing software such as Photoshop.[4] As a result, much of what is seen on social media is not necessarily a lie but is also not completely genuine.

Essena O'Neill, a nineteen-year-old Australian model, recounts her experience with the validation-culture of Instagram. Having gained over five hundred thousand followers, she was certainly not unnoticed in the realm of social media. Even so, she explains,

> Everyone goes through life differently, myself growing up with social comparing so easily available. It consumed me ... I spent [ages] 12–16 wishing I was someone else. Then I spent [ages] 16–19 constantly molding myself, editing and self-promoting the best parts of my life—which turned into a massive career based on numbers and how I looked aesthetically.... I simply no longer want to compare my life with anyone else's edited highlights. I want to put all of those hours I looked into a screen into my real-life goals, personal relationships, and aspirations. I'm over this celebrity culture and obsession. It's silly, and for the most part, intentionally lonely and fake.[5]

Here is a personal testimony of someone who has experienced all the fame and glory that social media has to offer, as well as the emptiness it creates inside. Chasing after temporary validation only creates a bigger hole to be filled.

Even worse, social media seems to be *creating* this need more than it is *fulfilling* the need. Donna Freitas explains, "People used to do things and *then* post them, and the approval you gained from whatever you were putting out there was a byproduct of the actual activity. Now the *anticipated* approval is what's driving the behavior or the activity, so there's just sort of been this reversal."[6] I was happy to hear O'Neill's decision to walk away from social media completely, especially having come to the stark realization at such a young age.

4. Kim, "Vivid Time Lapse," *Today*.
5. O'Neill, "Dear 12," YouTube.
6. Freitas, *The Happiness Effect*, 4.

Every other user being exposed to this façade of "beauty," then, has a new set of standards to live up to. This is why it is often so hard for young people to pick the right selfie; they want what they post to be perfect and to meet the guidelines of what is beautiful. Of course, this is not the case for all people on social media, but without a standard of beauty that does not change, which can only be found in the trustworthiness of God's unchanging Word, many people will fall into this trap of Satan. What happens when they cannot reach the false standard of beauty? They conclude that they must not be beautiful. This leads to depression and anger. Some studies have even concluded a correlation between taking selfies and narcissism among males[7] [8] and body-dissatisfaction and often depression among females.[9]

Even the simple feature known as "filters" has caused concern among many parents and even psychologists. A filter is a digital camera feature which adjusts the image captured by the camera by adjusting the hue, lighting, and even distorting the image or adding virtual reality to the person or object being viewed. For example, one of the most popular filters on Snapchat makes the user's face appear to have a dog nose and ears. When the person opens his or her mouth, the dog tongue appears and "licks the screen." It really is a fascinating feature. Another filter distorts your features, enlarging the eyes and making the nose and face thinner in order to appear "more attractive." While these filters may seem harmless, they ultimately feed into the narrative created by social media that we can only post the best versions of ourselves for others to see. In fact, many people are reluctant to post photos of themselves *unless* a filter is applied to the image, believing that they are in fact *unattractive without it.*

In fact, Instagram was recently under fire for featuring a "cosmetic surgery" filter, which, when applied, would display the

---

7. Sorokowski et al., "Selfie posting behaviors," *Personality and Individual Differences*, 123–127

8. Weiser, "#Me," *Personality and Individual Differences*, 477–481.

9. McLean et al., "Photoshopping the selfie," *International Journal of Eating Disorders*, 1132–1140.

markings that would be drawn onto one's face as if to direct the plastic surgeon where to make incisions and lift the facial features in a real cosmetic surgical procedure. What is disturbing about the filter is that it was called "FixMe." The idea is that there is an inherent issue with our appearance—with the face that God designed, and that this face needs to be fixed before it can be beautiful. Ironically, the filter's creator, Daniel Mooney, claimed that the filter was only ever created to critique the plastic surgery process, and that "perfection is overrated."

Sadly, many people took the filters all too seriously. Of recent times, young people have been taking screenshots of themselves with distorting filters applied to their faces and showing them to plastic surgeons to show them what they wish to look like, hoping the surgeon can recreate the digital image in real life. Are children and teenagers becoming the product of a system of me-ism that leads to detrimental views of themselves? I believe so. I am also convinced that the lies of the enemy are at the root of all of it.

Once value is attached to beauty, an endless pursuit of "attractiveness" will ensue. Young people must not become enslaved to the lies being thrown at them through the media.

Fasting from the Fast-Pace of Social Media

The only remedy, as I have already discussed, is the foundational truth of God's Word. It is beneficial, however, to take practical measures to avoid entrapment. Tony Reinke offers some practical ways we can avoid the shackles of personal technology. Here are 12 methods he lists:

1. Turn off all nonessential notifications.
2. Delete expired, nonessential, and time-wasting apps.
3. At night, keep your phone out of the bedroom.
4. Use a real alarm clock, not your phone alarm, to keep the phone out of your hands in the morning.

5. Guard your morning disciplines and evening sleep patterns by using phone settings to mute notifications between one hour before bedtime to a time when you can reasonably expect to be finished with personal disciplines in the morning.
6. Use self-restricting apps to help limit your smartphone functions and amount of time you invest in various platforms.
7. Recognize that much of what you respond to quickly can wait. Respond at a later, more convenient time.
8. Even if you need to *read* emails on your smartphone, use strategic points during the day to *respond* to emails at a computer.
9. Invite your spouse, your friends, and your family members to offer feedback on your phone habits.
10. When eating with your family members or friends, leave your phone out of sight.
11. When spending time with family members or friends, or when you are at church, leave your phone in a drawer, or in your car, or simply power it off.
12. At strategic moments in life, digitally detox your life and recalibrate your ultimate priorities. Step away from social media for frequent strategic stoppages, digital Sabbaths, and digital sabbaticals.[10]

Many of us become addicted to the sound of alerts on our phones. We must have them in our pockets at all times, and as soon as we hear the notification sound or feel the vibration of the phone, we hastily pull it out and check. More often than not, the notifications we get on a regular basis can wait. So, turn them off!

Take a break from social media. Your followers will still be there when you get back. In addition, there are plenty of other apps which we allow to drain valuable time from our days. Delete these to avoid being tempted to open them up at all.

As hard as it is to function regularly without our phones, we can suffice without them, I promise. Sometimes it takes putting

---

10. Reinke, *12 Ways Your Phone Is Changing You*, 200.

them away, out of sight to remember just how freeing life can be without constantly checking our phones. Don't get me wrong, I am not saying you should completely get rid of your phone; we live in a technology-driven culture. In fact, social media is an incredible tool for speaking freely, sharing ideas, and especially spreading the truth of the gospel! However, it helps to take time away from the screen every once in a while.

Predators

More frightening than psychological and emotional effects on social media users, however, is the prevalence of predators. Social media is simply another doorway through which they gain access to manipulating people. Ironically, in an age of "cyber-security," it seems as though our personal information is being distributed via the internet at rates higher than ever, and in ever-growing capacities. Media which promises its users safety actually opens many new and unexplored doors for child predators to wander through and into the homes of unknowing children.

A disturbing article written by Roo Powell, who uses the pseudonym Sloane Ryan, demonstrates the reality of this threat. The title of the article is "I'm a 37-Year-Old Mom & I Spent Seven Days Online as an 11-Year-Old Girl. Here's What I Learned."[11] Ryan was aided by a team, led by the CEO of an organization called Bark, which uses AI to alert parents when children are experiencing threats such as cyber-bullying and threats of violence. Ryan pretended to be an 11-year-old girl named Bailey and created a fake social media account to see how serious of a problem sexual predation really is. The results were enraging. She writes,

> At the beginning of the week, on the very first night as Bailey, two new messages came in under a minute after publishing a photo. We sat mouths agape as the numbers pinged up on the screen—2, 3, 7, 15 messages from adult men over the course of two hours. Half of them could be charged with transfer of obscene content to a

11. Ryan, "I'm A 37-Year-Old Mom," *Medium*.

minor. That night, I had taken a breather and sat with my head in my hands.

The article goes on to describe the various messages "Bailey" received, all from adult men, saying things like "I love your pictures on here. Does your mom and dad let you have a boyfriend yet," "you're so pretty," and "what would you do if you were here baby?" One man proceeds to ask for and describe sexual activities, as well as sending pictures and videos of such to the young girl. Ryan writes, "The brutal reality is that a predator doesn't have to be in the same room, building, or even country to abuse a child. And that's what they're doing—subjecting children to psychological and sexual abuse."

Sexual predators are real and active on social media. Ernie Allen, president and CEO of the National Center for Missing and Exploited Children says, "Predators are hiding behind the anonymity of the Internet to target kids, to entice kids online—to try to persuade them to meet them in the physical world." This is a heartbreaking reality. Crimes Against Children Research Center concludes that *1 in 5 children* who log onto the internet say they have received unwanted sexual solicitation via the Web. Solicitations were defined as requests to engage in sexual activities or sexual talk, or to give personal sexual information. Likewise, in 27 percent of incidents of sexual exploitation via the internet, predators asked children for sexual photos of themselves.[12] Finally, more than 50 percent of online sexual exploitation victims are between the ages of 12 and 15. So, just how easy is it for predators to get a hold of children online?

A University of New Hampshire report on sexual predators describes the methods of sexual predators in this way:

> The research about Internet-initiated sex crimes makes it clear that the stereotype of the Internet child molester who uses trickery and violence to assault children is largely inaccurate (Wolak, Finkelhor & Mitchell, 2004). Most Internet-initiated sex crimes involve adult men who use the Internet to meet and seduce underage

12. Wolak et al., American Psychologist, 63, 111-128.

adolescents into sexual encounters. The offenders use Internet communications such as instant messages, e-mail, and chatrooms to meet and develop intimate relationships with victims. In the great majority of cases, victims are aware they are conversing online with adults. In the N-JOV Study, only 5% of offenders pretended to be teens when they met potential victims online (Wolak et al., 2004).[13]

The most obvious and common method is, as we have already discussed, the seemingly limitless possibilities of social media. Though sites have gradually become more cautious and aware of the type of profiles created on their servers, the option for creating a fake social media profile is always available. A CBS Boston article featured an example of this. The author wrote,

> The Boston FBI assisted in the arrest and conviction of a man in England, who blackmailed a 13-year-old girl from Massachusetts. The girl thought she was corresponding on Facebook with a young man and sent him a naked picture; it was actually a 35-year-old man named Jonathan Murphy. He threatened the girl that he would come to the U.S. if she didn't send him more pictures. The family reported him to the FBI and he is now behind bars.[14]

However, websites exist which allow users to connect with complete strangers without having to create a fake identity—and even live video-chat with them!

Omegle is a popular website aimed exactly at what I just described. In fact, the tagline for the website is, "talk to strangers!" Omegle accesses the user's webcam or phone camera to connect him or her with a complete stranger at random. Once the video-chat is live and the two are connected, they can talk about or do whatever they choose. There is also the chat option, which simply allows users to type that which they wish to say to whichever stranger with which they have been connected. The danger of Omegle is not difficult to predict—anyone doing anything could be on the opposite

---

13. Wolak et al., "Online Predators."
14. Anderson, "FBI," *CBS Boston.*

side of the camera. You run your own risk when being connected at random with a stranger. There is no way of predicting whether you will be faced with a man or woman with no clothes on, often pleasuring themselves on camera.

Of course, users can choose to only be connected to those with whom they share 'common interests;' this allows users to type in interests, and they will only be connected with someone who has typed in the same things. However, this method only increases the likelihood of a predator being connected with exactly who he or she is looking for.

Even the Omegle website is abundantly aware of these risks. While the website asks that only users 18-years-old or older be allowed on the website, we have seen with porn websites that these guidelines are rarely, if ever followed. This is what the home page of Omegle now says:

> Omegle *(oh·meg·ull)* is a great way to meet new friends. When you use Omegle, we pick someone else at random and let you talk one-on-one. To help you stay safe, chats are anonymous unless you tell someone who you are (not suggested!), and you can stop a chat at any time. Predators have been known to use Omegle, so please be careful.

Essentially, they are making everyone who visits the website aware: *there is an extreme likelihood that by using this website you could be putting yourself at risk of being connected to a predator.* It is imperative that parents know who their children are connected with on social media. Please be starkly clear with children about the dangers of online predators. Also, be clear that predators *often* do not appear as predators. Otherwise, even young children would be more apt to discern their intent. They disguise themselves as trustworthy people, often claiming to be a friend of the family. Many will even disguise themselves as reputable people within society, such as *youth pastors*. This way, even parents may be deceived into trusting them.

Entire YouTube channels exist devoted to exposing sexual predators. Many users set up scenarios which appear to be real, but are really posing as underage girls and boys, and the sexual predators are eager to pursue immoral and illegal acts with them. These YouTube users do a great job of demonstrating just how easy it is for predators to contact young girls and boys to try and coerce them into sex, and just how forward they can often be with their demands. In addition, MSNBC aired the television series, *To Catch a Predator*, in which a group of investigators would go undercover to set up local sexual predators and display the realities and dangers of the traps many children and teenagers can fall into if not warned and taught how to discern.

The tactics of deception invoked by predators is nothing new or unique. Our enemy, the devil, operates in this very way as well. Paul writes to the Corinthians, "For such men are false apostles, deceitful workers, disguising themselves as apostles of Christ. No wonder, for even Satan disguises himself as an angel of light. Therefore, it is not surprising if his servants also disguise themselves as servants of righteousness, whose end will be according to their deeds" (2 Corinthians 11:13–15). This is why discernment in the life of the believer is so crucial. Otherwise, we will be driven by the lust of what looks good and pleasurable but will ultimately end in our demise as a trap from the Enemy.

Test everything! Be watchful! Be aware—and clear—about the risks of unrestricted access to the internet with children and teenagers. For practical purposes, there is a software called ScreenRetriever, which allows parents to monitor activity happening on their children's devices. This will make you more aware of the potential monsters your child may be exposed to. There is also a software called Bark, which provides similar protection and monitoring; however, the best way to ensure protection against predators is to lay out the realities of their existence and how to avoid them. Chat rooms, especially coupled with online flirting, can be very dangerous. Children and teenagers should also know that they should never post any sensitive personal information to the internet or revealing pictures that would not normally be shared with friends or family.

Tinder

There is not much to say about Tinder; that is, if you already know what it is. If you do not, allow me to briefly explain. Tinder is not a typical dating app. Rather; it is predominately used for "hook-ups." That is, Tinder provides users with a way to meet people for the strict purpose of sex. The sad truth, however, is that most within our culture will not view this as a bad thing. American culture has adopted the lie that sex is merely transactional and exists for the sole purpose of pleasure. This is exactly what Tinder seeks to provide users.

Nancy Pearcy describes this trend of sexual encounters as "Hookup Culture" in her book *Love Thy Body*. It completely removes any relational aspect of the relationship. Unfortunately, it is becoming increasingly common and accepted. Without the truth of a Biblical view of sexuality, why would anyone object to such a view of meaningless sex? This is the type of culture that Paul alludes to in Romans 1 when describing the idolatry people choose to follow, while suppressing the truth of God. He says,

> Professing to be wise, they became fools, and exchanged the glory of the incorruptible God for an image in the form of corruptible man and of birds and four-footed animals and crawling creatures.
>
> Therefore God gave them over in the lusts of their hearts to impurity, so that their bodies would be dishonored among them. For they exchanged the truth of God for a lie, and worshiped and served the creature rather than the Creator, who is blessed forever. Amen.
>
> For this reason God gave them over to degrading passions; for their women exchanged the natural function for that which is unnatural, and in the same way also the men abandoned the natural function of the woman and burned in their desire toward one another, men with men committing indecent acts and receiving in their own persons the due penalty of their error.

Paul says that this kind of unrepentant sin and sexual immorality is what invokes the wrath of God. We must teach a true view of sexuality if we are going to raise up a generation of people who will not depart from the faith and will be willing to defend it with reverence and love.

Not to mention, Tinder is another perfect outlet for sexual predators. Understand that the app is often not used just for sex; defenders of it will most likely argue against what I am writing here. However, sexual encounters are the primary goal of users who download the app. It allows people to view another person's profile, and if they do not find interest in the person, they may "swipe right," causing the app to show them someone else whose profile potentially matches their interests. Understand the ease-of-access so many teenagers now have concerning sexual encounters and potential "relationships." The danger is, of course, not knowing whether every profile is legitimate.

10

Demons and Suicide Games

IN 2016, A CHALLENGE surfaced on the internet called "Blue Whale." Internet challenges were, and still are, a popular fad among children and teenagers. One of the first ones I remember was the cinnamon challenge. This involved attempting to swallow a spoonful of cinnamon, which is easier said than done. As more challenges became known, they also became more extreme. Blue Whale was supposedly a game that users could play which involved carrying out 50 "tasks" in a matter of 50 days, the last of which being suicide.

BBC News posted an article detailing what is known about the challenge. Ant Adeane writes,

> The story of the Blue Whale challenge began with Rina Palenkova. On 22 November 2015, Rina, a teenager living in south-eastern Russia, posted a selfie. In the photo she is standing outside. A black scarf is wrapped around her mouth and nose. She is sticking her middle finger up at the camera. It looks like it's covered in dried blood. The photo's caption read: "Nya bye". The next day, she took her own life.[1]

According to the report, Palenkova's death was discussed on a chat room hosted by Russia's largest social network, VKontakte.

---

1. Adeane, "Blue Whale," *BBC News*.

In this forum, teenagers often discussed topics such as suicide and depression. Not long after the suicide of Palenkova, two other teenagers took their own lives as well; the one thing they all had in common was posts on similar chat groups containing mentions of blue whales shortly before their suicides.

Eventually, as similar events continued occurring, blue whales became a national topic of concern in Russia. The report continues,

> An article by journalist Galina Mursalieva in Novaya Gazeta, an investigative newspaper, sent the story into overdrive. Mursalieva suggested that inside certain online groups, some of them with enigmatic names like "Ocean Whales" and "f57", existed a game. In this game, so-called "curators" would set players 50 tasks over 50 days. On the last day the user was instructed to take their own life. The Novaya Gazeta report estimated that 130 children might have killed themselves between November 2015 and April 2016 because of their participation in these groups. It would come to be known worldwide as the Blue Whale challenge.

Eventually, 21-year-old Philipp Budeikin was found to be behind the "game," and was arrested for inciting teenagers to commit suicide. This demonstrates the power of influence that one person can have via the internet.

A similar incident occurred more recently; this one was not in Russia, however. The "Momo Challenge" surfaced in 2019. It featured a photo of a very disturbing sculpture called "Mother Bird," created by Japanese artist Keisuke Aiso. Though it turned out to be a hoax, the challenge did create significant hysteria among many parents and news outlets.

Supposedly, "Momo" was a demon that possessed certain messaging apps, primarily one called WhatsApp, and featured the scary image along with instructions for children to carry out tasks. Should they refuse or fail to complete the tasks, Momo would threaten to kill them. Some of the tasks involved self-harm or harm to others. Sophie Lewis of CBS News wrote this concerning the Momo Challenge:

> Law enforcement also says parents need to focus on the bigger picture: "Even basic open source research suggests that 'Momo' is run by hackers who are looking for personal info," PSNI Craigavon wrote on Facebook. "The danger lies with your child feeling pressured to either follow the orders of ANY app via 'challenges,' or peer pressure in chat rooms and the like . . . More important is that your child knows not to give out personal info to ANYONE they don't know, that no one has the right to tell them to, or make them do ANYTHING they don't want to."[2]

Though no real instances of suicide were related to the supposed challenge, it does say a lot about the ability for internet hoaxes to be spread. Even the very idea that so many believed the hoax suggests how easy it is for lies (frightening ones at that) to be spread throughout the internet. I must say, when I first saw the challenge, I believed it could in fact be true, being that I was already familiar with the Blue Whale challenge as well.

Despite the majority of news articles saying things like, "The Momo Challenge Is Not Real" (*The Atlantic*), "Momo Challenge: Please Don't Worry About It. Here's Why" (*CNN*), and "The bogus 'Momo challenge' internet hoax, explained" (*Vox*), it did spark fear in many parents and children. In fact, one article describes a mother named Pearl Woods, who claims that her daughter did, in fact, have an encounter with Momo. The article reads,

> Woods, who lives in Folsom, is careful about what videos her daughter, Zoey, can watch online and has multiple parental settings. "She's on the spectrum and a lot of children that are, are very impressionable," she said. A few weeks ago, Zoey began displaying some unusual behavior. "Where is 'suicide' coming from? Why would she ask me about a knife into an outlet?" Woods said. Last weekend Zoey turned the kitchen gas stove

---

2. Lewis, "Police issue warning," *CBS News*.

on without letting it light, which created a potentially explosive situation. "She kept telling me about Momo and I just didn't understand, I see now," Woods said. She discovered alarming short clips popping up in the videos Zoey was watching. "She pauses the screen as soon as I walked in and I saw this creepy masked doll looking," Woods said. Her daughter told her, "It was Momo making bad videos. It was bad."[3]

A YouTube spokesperson claimed that YouTube guidelines prohibit the type of content involving dangerous challenges, as were suspected to be the content of the supposed Momo videos. However, many similar claims arose concerning the Momo challenge. "Blue Whale" was heartbreakingly real; could there have been some truth to the Momo challenge as well?

Teaching Children How to Conjure Up Demons

Regardless of the validity of Momo, perhaps demonic activity stemming from the media is not a "hoax" after all. The concept of spiritual warfare is often scoffed at or mocked as ridiculous and false. On the opposite side of the spectrum, many observe the reality of demonic activity. Entire religions and churches are devoted to worshipping the devil. Multiple religious cults exist such as the Church of Satan, the Satanic Temple, the Order of Nine Angels, etc. So, demonic activity is becoming increasingly "normal" within our culture. If you are still skeptical, just look at some of the literature being sold to children.

There is a book which was published by Aaron Leighton in July of 2019, titled *A Children's Book of Demons*. The book teaches children that "summoning demons has never been so much fun," and tells them how to conjure up demons and make them a part of their lives. Right away, many will look at this and think *Okay, Adam, now that is a bit extreme. Certainly, this book is just a playful*

---

3. CBS News, "Momo Challenge."

approach to spiritual activity. I mean, are you going to come after people who read and watch Harry Potter?

I want to be very clear that, regardless of how serious or "playful" this topic may be passed off as, it should not be accepted that way. Demonic activity is very real, and this is simply one of many examples of how Satan can sneak into the mainstream culture and lead people (in this case, children) astray from the truth of God. In response to the objection about Harry Potter, it is important to note that witchcraft is very prevalent as well. According to a survey conducted by Pew Research Center in 2008, there were more Wiccans in America than Presbyterians! Voodoo dolls are even being sold in retail stores. This rise of wickedness should not be hard to believe; after all, we were specifically warned about this in 2 Timothy 3:13. "But evil men and impostors will proceed from bad to worse, deceiving and being deceived."

Even a recent Disney Channel TV show features demonic activity as if it is mainstream (which, as we have just seen, it now is). The show is called "The Owl House," and features a teenage girl named Luz who stumbles upon a mystical world and meets a witch named Eda. She then enters into various adventures featuring sorcery, demons, and witches, while learning how to be a witch herself.

Of course, this is not the first Disney show, or children's show in general, to feature demonic activity and witchcraft. Even so, many Christian parents pushed back on the concept, with good reason. The show makes light of real topics such as hell and demons. Inviting demonic media into the home should never be embraced nonchalantly. Not so surprisingly, many people mocked the fact that Christian parents were hesitant to let their children watch the show. Understand that I am not against watching media that features witchcraft, because there are probably some readers who started thinking "are you saying we can't watch Harry Potter?" No, but we need to be abundantly clear that much of what we see in said movies and TV shows is very real. *And they are not of God* (Isaiah 8:19-22). The Bible tells us to avoid witchcraft and demonic activity of any sort (Deuteronomy 18:10-11). I will leave it up to the parent to discern what should be viewed for entertainment purposes and what should not be allowed to enter the home.

Understand that these lies are being accepted by the media and majority of culture; in order to put an end to them, we must be able to discern them. There is a spiritual battle happening as you are reading this, and the Bible makes abundantly clear the reality of demonic activity and possession. 1 Timothy 4:1 says, "But the Spirit explicitly says that in later times some will fall away from the faith, paying attention to deceitful spirits and doctrines of demons." We are undoubtedly living in these times today. The heartbreaking reality is that these spiritual forces are at play in the lives of children as well. There is a fundamental need for believers to guard our hearts and minds (Philippians 4:7).

Part 3: **Indoctrination**

11

Attack on Christianity

I MENTIONED AT THE beginning of this book that I am part of Generation Z. I also mentioned the stark contrast between my generation and previous generations. I firmly believe we will be the first generation in history to have grown up considering the aforementioned topics and those which I am about to delve into as "status quo." And it breaks my heart to admit that. But I cannot deny the reality of the state of the culture, and of the rate of apostasy among believers.

So, the question arises: *how did we get here?*

We are in the middle of a crisis; it is one which has been going on for many decades and will not let up any time soon. America is facing a significant moral decline. However, I believe there are deeper, unseen forces at play, as is the case with every matter of all times. I am speaking of a demonic presence among the nation right now. There is a war going on, but it is not one of flesh and blood (Ephesians 6:12). No, this is a battle of spiritual forces. I am not arguing from one side or another; I am merely pointing out the fact that there are very real forces at play that many of us do not realize.

What does any of this have to do with the monsters in the closet we have been discussing thus far in this book? The answer is plain: the one thing all these pervasive threats have had in common is *spiritual* and even, I would argue, *demonic* activity. Right now, we are seeing the work of the enemy in the lives of young people through the use of indoctrination. If Satan can destroy the foundation of truth, he can convince people of anything that opposes the authority of God's Word. In this section, I will evaluate some of the most egregious lies being pushed in our culture today. Depending on how "woke" you are, some of these may come as a surprise to you, but I promise you everything you are about to read is 100 percent real and there are people who 100 percent believe some of the egregious narratives, and will go to great lengths to ensure your children believe them as well.

The War on Biblical Values

Recently, an article was published from *Harvard Law Review,* titled "The Risks of Homeschooling," by Erin O'Donnell. The article seeks to suggest that homeschooling, as an alternative to public school, is more harmful than it is helpful. As one who was homeschooled for most of elementary and middle school, I wanted to know what the author had to say. One quote jumped out at me. Regarding the reasons for which parents choose to homeschool, O'Donnell writes, "surveys of homeschoolers show that a majority of homeschoolers (by some estimates, up to 90 percent) are driven by conservative Christian beliefs, and seek to remove their children from mainstream culture."[1] Of course, O'Donnell paints conservatism in a bad light, but ironically argues that children should grow up being taught to tolerate other people's viewpoints. One wonders why she does not tolerate the conservative viewpoint. At any rate, the article sheds light on a stark reality of our time: Biblical values are under attack.

O'Donnell, in a follow-up article comprised of questions and answers with Elizabeth Bartholet, writes this:

---

1. O'Donnell, "The Risks of Homeschooling." *Harvard Magazine.*

ATTACK ON CHRISTIANITY

> Behind the rapid growth of the homeschooling movement is the growth in the conservative evangelical movement. Conservative Christians wanted the chance to bring their children up with their values and belief systems and saw homeschooling as a way to escape from the secular education in public schools. They had fought the battle with public school systems to have their children exempted from exposure to alternative values in the schools and lost. When they started withdrawing their children for homeschooling, this propelled expansion of the homeschooling movement.[2]

The interesting fact is that she is not entirely wrong. Many parents' motivation for homeschooling is, in fact, to provide a Biblical foundation of knowledge and truth, with good reason. However, the entire premise of her article is that this is harmful to children, and that homeschooling ultimately should not be an option. Biblical values are not tolerated in modern society; it is time to press forward harder than ever before with regards to the truth of scripture in contrast to the lies being spouted off by the media and the education system. In this section, I will evaluate some of the major narratives saturating both media and education, which children and teenagers are being fed.

---

2. Mineo, "A warning on homeschooling." *The Harvard Gazette.*

12

Abortion

Disclaimer: I am not going to make a case against abortion here. I will make the immorality of it abundantly clear, but this section is simply pointing out some of the extreme positions people take about abortion, and the narrative being pushed by the culture. For answers to common objections, see the Appendix.

IN 1973, THE SUPREME Court Case, Roe vs Wade was passed, which legalized abortion. Since then, roughly 50 million babies have been killed by abortion. Hundreds of thousands lose their life every year because of it. Approximately 3,000 babies are killed in America every day due to abortion, and these occur roughly every 90 seconds at a Planned Parenthood facility alone.

The Centers for Disease Control and Prevention (CDC) defines abortion as "an intervention performed by a licensed clinician (e.g., a physician, nurse-midwife, nurse practitioner, physician assistant) within the limits of state regulations that is intended to terminate a suspected or known ongoing intrauterine pregnancy and that does not result in a live birth." The argument being made by those who are "pro-choice" is that abortion should remain legal, because it is a right. After all, if the baby is a part of the woman's body, should she not be able to decide whether to give birth to the child? Tragically, narratives against saving the lives of unborn children are becoming louder and louder in the United States.

Again, I am not going to go into a deep case against abortion here. I do, however, want to point out how extreme some of the pro-choice arguments are becoming. It is imperative that we define abortion for what it really is: abortion is killing an unborn child while he or she is still in the mother's womb.

First, it is important to realize the flaw in the predominant argument being made by those who consider themselves pro-choice. The idea of "pro-choice" actually reduces the pre-born child to merely a part of the mother's body. "I should be allowed to *choose* what I do with *my body*." This is intentional, being that if you can reduce the child to a "clump of cells," as many pro-abortion advocates argue, you have eradicated the humanity of the child. Once the child is no longer a human being in the minds of people, this makes the murder of the child much less immoral. After all, what is the immorality of removing a clump of cells from the body?

The problem with the clump of cells argument is that it commits a logical fallacy known as "begging the question." Begging the question means that one is assuming a conclusion within one or more premises; in other words, begging the question means assuming a truth about the claim you are advocating for, without real evidence or proof to support said claim. Many pro-abortion advocates beg the question that the pre-born child, or fetus, is not actually a human person, and therefore abortion is not wrong.

This is the primary narrative being fed to children and teenagers. If, however, the child is in fact a human being, then he or she deserves the right to life as well. This would negate abortion as the right of the mother; after all, there is another person's life which is now in the question as well. So many of those on the side of abortion refuse to acknowledge this truth. We must be willing to accept the stark reality of abortion: abortion is mass genocide. In fact, as the Guttmacher Institute concludes, in 2017, there were approximately 862,320 abortions. *That is 862,320 innocent children murdered.* There is a fantastic pro-life organization I follow and support called Live Action. They work hard to provide scientific evidence, statistics, and philosophical truths against abortion. They also expose some of the atrocities of the abortion industry, and the corrupt "women's rights" organizations such as Planned Parenthood. Please check them out.

Recently, a comedian by the name of Michelle Wolf, who has a comedy special on Netflix, said this about her own abortion:

> "A lot of people think that even if you're allowed to get abortions, it should only be for a very few, specific reasons. Well, I think you should be able to get an abortion for any reason you want . . . You can feel any way you want after an abortion. Get one! See how you feel . . . You know how my abortion made me feel? Very powerful. You know how people say you can't play God? . . . I walked out of there being like, 'Move over, Morgan Freeman, I am God.'"[1]

"I am God." Even though this is a joke (in poor taste) from a comedy act, something about that fact makes it even harder to stomach; abortion has become the subject of stand-up comedy. The argument for abortion used to be "safe, legal, and rare;" now it seems as though advocates are screaming it from the rooftops. In fact, for many abortion organizations, this is exactly what they wish to achieve. Take the group known as "Shout Your Abortion," for instance. The group focuses on making abortion a praise-worthy act and encouraging those who have had abortions to celebrate. Here is the information on the front page of their website:

> *Shout Your Abortion* is a collection of photos, essays, and creative work inspired by the movement of the same name, a template for building new communities of healing, and a call to action. Since SYA's inception, people all over the country begun sharing stories and organizing in a range of ways: making art, hosting comedy shows, creating abortion-positive clothing, altering billboards, and starting conversations that had never happened before. This book documents some of these projects and individuals who have breathed life into

---

1. Wolf, "Joke Show," *Netflix*.

this movement, illustrating the profound liberatory and political power of defying shame and claiming sole authorship of our experiences.[2]

Nothing is hidden; they are brutally honest about the narrative they wish to spread through this organization. I found it increasingly difficult to scroll down that same page of the website; I was coming across headlines for articles such as "abortion is for everyone," "I've had 5 abortions," and even "I felt bad for not feeling bad." My heart broke; these are real stories from real women who have been fed the lie that abortion is something to be celebrated, and that no one suffers. But as I was scrolling, I could not help but imagine the number of innocent babies whose lives had been stolen, and now have an entire webpage dedicated to the decisions their mothers made to end them.

Abortion's Media Presence

In February of 2020, a disturbing TikTok video surfaced and eventually went viral, thankfully for the sheer reason that so many people were appalled by its message. The video features two young women, probably college age, with the headline "Abortion time! TAKE 2" at the beginning. The video cuts to the girls sitting in a car outside of a Planned Parenthood facility, and the girl who was presumably having the abortion giggles as the camera pans to her face. The caption reads, "nervous laugh." The next scene, inside the waiting room, reveals another couple with their heads down, and the caption, "There's two abortion moods." The camera pans to the girl who will be having the abortion; she is doing a dance in her seat and smiling. Finally, the girl is seen smiling as she is sitting in the medical chair, after which the camera pans to display the ultrasound of her child. Thankfully, the video ends here, though how the story ended is obvious to the viewers. I was blown away when I saw the video.

2. Taken from https://shoutyourabortion.com/book/

PART 3: INDOCTRINATION

Lila Rose, founder of Live Action, tweeted concerning the video, "Our ability to be cruel is endless. When society celebrates abortion, should we be surprised to see this kind of cruelty? My heart breaks for this little helpless baby, killed on camera, his young mother joking about it. And it breaks for her, who will live with this all her life." This casual, nonchalant approach to abortion is not unique to that video; in fact, TikTok, the popular social media platform among teenagers today, seems to be a hotbed for the topic of celebratory abortion. I came across another video featuring the title, "reasons why abortion is not okay." A girl is pictured in the video, and several reasons appear around her as music is playing. One by one, different phrases appear on the screen, including, "It's a human," "It's murder," "It has a beating heart," "A fetus has a right to live," "The baby can just go to foster care," and finally, "It's not the woman's body, it's a real human." The girl in the video then pretends to shoot away each reason, and mouths the words, *"there's not any."*

I was surprised at how many videos were titled, "abortion time," and simply featured women in abortion facilities smiling and often dancing before the procedures took place. Lastly, I found plenty of videos saying things such as "don't like abortion? Then don't get one! But don't take away my right." *That would be like saying, "don't like slavery? Then don't own a slave! But don't take away my right,"* or *"don't like murder? Then don't commit one! Don't like theft? Then don't steal!"*

Many of the videos I found were so disturbing that I cannot even describe them here. On top of that, there were plenty factually incorrect narratives and statistics about abortion, though this is to be expected being that it is public social media domain. However, the fact that so many children and teenagers are being faced with these egregious videos daily is a heartbreaking reality.

Though many deny the fact, this is the narrative being pushed by so many abortion advocates and feminists alike—there is a feeling of power and entitlement to having the right to kill an unborn child. There are even candles being sold with the label, *abortion is magical.* This is the understanding many teenagers (and even children) will buy into, which is why they are putting colloquial descriptive terms such as *magical* to describe a brutal medical procedure. If abortion really is simply the removal of a part of the woman's body, as abortion advocates claim, why does this particular procedure require so much promotion? Of course, they would answer by saying this is because those who are pro-life are attempting to revoke their rights to choose. Therefore, such promotion of the choice is necessary in order to persuade more people to be pro-abortion. However, no one should have the "right" to choose to murder an innocent child.

This should serve as a sign that, though many want to eradicate any feelings of remorse from taking the lives of innocent babies, the moral law is in fact written on our hearts. As Paul writes to the Christians in Rome, "For when Gentiles, who do not have the law, by nature do what the law requires, they are a law to themselves, even though they do not have the law. They show that the work of the law is written on their hearts, while their conscience also bears witness, and their conflicting thoughts accuse or even excuse them on that day when, according to my gospel, God judges the secrets of men by Christ Jesus" (Romans 2:14–16). So, the fact that so many extremist abortion groups are trying to erase any negative feelings from having an abortion should not deter us from what God's Word says; we know the truth, but we choose to suppress it.

> *Certainly, the education system is not telling children that abortion is something to be celebrated, right?*

You would be surprised. The organization known as *Safe2Choose* has an article on their website about this very topic. The author writes,

> We all know that information is power, but abortion is so stigmatized that people are often trying to avoid bringing it up, hoping it will cease to happen if nobody says the word. However, abortion has been happening since the beginning of time, and is one of the most common medical procedures still to this day—1 in 3 women will have an abortion throughout their lifetime. We need to give our

kids all the tools they need to navigate their sexual world safely. School is where students start shaping their own identity and opinion on many subjects—often different from their parents' grip—and the education system owes them scientific and non-judgmental information along with a safe space to engage these questions.[3]

If we do not act now, this idea will become mainstream, and pro-life voices will be silenced (as is already the case for many).

On the contrary, schools that do teach what abortion really is, and the gruesome procedures involved therein, are often condemned. One California schoolteacher in particular received backlash for showing a now frequently viewed video from former abortionist, Dr. Anthony Levatino, who describes in detail the process of abortion and how it ultimately dismembers and destroys a fetus. This video was shown to students as a response to a state law which had been recently passed requiring schools to provide comprehensive sexual education. Whether this particular video was too graphic or not, I do believe the reality of abortion should be spoken and not hidden. The University of Southern California concluded, however, that only *13 of the 50 states* in the nation require sex education to be medically accurate![4] Teenagers and young people need to know the truth about abortion.

This is perhaps one of the reasons Planned Parenthood is so reluctant to allow mothers the opportunity to view and listen to the ultra-sounds of their children. They are aware of the possibility of the mother realizing the humanity of the child, and then choosing not to follow through with an abortion. In fact, most Planned Parenthood facilities do not even provide basic prenatal care![5] Investigators from pro-life group Live Action went to 97 different Planned

---

3. Diaz, "The role of schools," Safe2Choose.org.

4. University of Southern California, "America's Sex Education."

5. Watch this shocking video revealed by Live Action: https://www.youtube.com/watch?v=ekgiScr364Y&feature=youtu.be See also the blog post written about it: https://www.liveaction.org/defund-debate-hits-live-action-exposes-planned-parenthoods-prenatal-care-deception/

Parenthood locations and were *turned away by 92 of them.*[6] Live Action has done much more extensive research into Planned Parenthood than just this. I highly advise you to look into some of the devastating conclusions they have reached.

Christian Discipleship and Abortion

Understand this: abortion is not just a political issue. It is a moral issue that is presented as a political issue. When discipling children, we must make that much clear. In fact, all laws legislate morality. The only question is *whose* morality will be legislated? Tony Perkins says this about the abortion issue: "The abortion debate is far more than a mere political issue. It strikes at the heart of every society. Without the light of God's Word upholding the sanctity of human life, Western nations lose all respect for the sanctity of the unborn."[7] The unborn are sacred lives worth saving. This is why so many pro-life organizations such as *Live Action* and *Students for Life* are devoted this very task.

If the Scriptures are true, and I believe that they are, then we as the body of Christ have an obligation to preserve the sanctity of life. In fact, James says "So whoever knows the right thing to do and fails to do it, for him it is sin" (James 4:17). Remaining silent about the issue of abortion is sin. We as the church must speak up and speak the truth unashamedly. We must also teach our children the truth as well—if not, the media and public education systems will tell them otherwise. Will the church be willing to fight for those who cannot fight for themselves? I pray that we will someday look back on history and ask the question, "what were we thinking?" However, I also pray that we look back and remember it was the body of Christ who stood for the life of the unborn.

---

6. See the full list here: https://www.liveaction.org/wp-content/uploads/2017/01/PP-centers-investigated-for-prenatal-care-1.pdf

7. Perkins, "Fighting Abortion," *Answers in Genesis*.

PART 3: INDOCTRINATION

There is Hope

I do not wish to paint a completely disheartening picture of the state of the nation; I do, however, believe it is crucial that we are aware of what is happening. We cannot turn a blind eye to the millions of children being murdered, and the voices trying to justify this. There is hope, though!

Like the organizations mentioned earlier, pro-life groups are hard at work to end the violence of abortion. I cannot tell you how many real-life stories I read on a regular basis of mothers who had the opportunity to abort their child, but decided to birth him or her instead, and the joy that ensued. They are often overwhelmed by the sheer happiness of being able to hold the baby in their arms which almost did not get the chance to live!

I mentioned the influence which the pro-choice narrative has on TikTok, but there is also a significant pro-life presence there as well. In fact, typing "abortion" in the search bar of TikTok seemed to display an equal search result of pro-choice and pro-life videos. This is inspiring. It demonstrates that while it may be easy to lose hope in the younger generation, many of them are leading the way in moral rightness for their peers. They are also realizing the impact they can create on social media. With close to 100 thousand followers on TikTok, Live Action also regularly creates encouraging content in defense of the unborn!

In addition, organizations such as the American Center for Law and Justice (ACJL) are actively fighting back against abortion groups and fighting for life. Save The Storks is another pro-life group that offers counseling for abortion-minded women and is available to talk with them if they have any regrets about their decision. They often set up their "stork bus" outside of abortion facilities to raise advocacy, awareness, and options to pregnant women who may be terrified of where their lives could go next.

Similarly, for every abortion facility, there are approximately two crisis pregnancy centers. These exist to provide options to pregnant women who may be considering abortion, or who do not know where to turn. Many offer free ultrasounds to abortion-minded women, considering taking the life of the child. One example is Life Line Pregnancy Center, located in Wilmington, NC, whose success rate for having shown the ultrasound technology to pregnant women is *94 percent!*

Pregnant women need to know that abortion is not the answer; some sources conclude that there are as many as *36 families* waiting to adopt for every *1 pregnancy* in the United States. Yes, there is hope for the unborn! And this is a reason *not* to give up hope, but to keep fighting back and raising awareness about the realities of abortion so that children and teenagers are not lied to by the enemy. Time and time again, people are learning the truth about the unborn—that neither size, nor stage of development, nor sentience, nor the fact that the child is not wanted, nor the idea that the child would be a burden, can eradicate the value which God has given that precious human being.

Recommended Resources

The Case for Life: Equipping Christians to Engage the Culture by Scott Klusendorf

Pro-Life Answers to Pro-Choice Arguments by Randy Alcorn

Legislating Morality: Is It Wise? Is It Legal? Is It Possible? by Norman Geisler and Frank Turek

Love Thy Body: Answering Hard Questions About Life and Sexuality by Nancy Pearcey

13

Sexuality

Disclaimer: for a more detailed analysis of this topic, I have added a list of recommended resources at the end of this section devoted specifically to sexuality from a Biblical standpoint. Also, for answers to common objections, see the Appendix.

THERE IS NO QUESTION that the very definition of sexuality, and thus marriage, is being challenged by the culture as we speak. In fact, it seems as though every day, the number of people who support a traditional view of marriage is decreasing tremendously. Gallop Polls shows that, since 2006, the support for same-sex marriage to be recognized legally has consistently increased, after having varied over the previous decades. Today, roughly 73 percent of the people surveyed are in support of same-sex marriage, while a mere 26 percent are not. Likewise, as of 2011, the number of people in support of equal marriage rights for same-sex couples has been consistently higher than those which are against them, whose numbers have significantly decreased.

Again, this should not come as a surprise to anyone; but the redefinition of sexuality does not stop there. Only recently has the transgender[1] movement been so prevalent in our culture, and

---

1. Transgenderism is the ideology that biological "gender" is not equivalent to sex but is purely subjective according to the individual's preference. If

it frightens me how quickly it was adopted. In fact, trans-rights seemed to come out of nowhere. Even radical feminists are pushing back against the extreme requests being pushed by the transgender community. We will dive into some of these shortly. First, however, it is vital to have a grasp on what is really happening here.

The Sexual Revolution Is Not About Sex

The late Mike Adams, a former professor at University of North Carolina Wilmington, commented on a question asked about the transgender bathroom debate at an apologetics conference called "Fearless Faith." He responded to the topic by saying this:

> One of the things that bothers me about this the most is that the American Psychological Association—it has become such a political lobby. And isn't it interesting that around 1972, they lobbied, not based upon scientific breakthrough, but simply through political maneuvering, to say that homosexuality is no longer an emotional or psychological disorder, and then they move on to the next thing. And it's gender identity. Did anyone notice that no sooner did they declassify those things as being mental illnesses that they started to develop new terms and circulate them in the court of public opinion? We had, all of a sudden, "homophobia." Now we have "transphobia." Something goes from being a disorder, and then suddenly the next day, any opposition to it is a psychological disorder. Make no mistake about it: these individuals are trying to say that your Christian worldview is a psychological disorder. This is war. And understand, it is a war of competing worldviews. And we need to understand that this whole thing is not about where the

---

a girl "identifies" as a boy, then society must affirm that identity for her. Her biological markers are not relevant; what matters is what she claims. Likewise, it follows that the traditional pronouns associated with a sex (he/his, her/hers) are not standard either. Rather, one may choose his or her own pronouns, and all people are (often legally) obliged to conform to said preference.

PART 3: INDOCTRINATION

> transgendered pee; it is about postmodernism and the
> question of whether things have essences.²

"This whole thing is not about where the transgendered pee." I found that to be an incredibly insightful statement. The entire debate really boils down to one question: *what does it mean to be human?* If that question is free for us to define however we please, then we should expect movements such as transgenderism, same-sex relationships, and every post-modern ideal. That is what we get when we look at the world through the lens of our own desires. However, if we look at our desires through the lens of truth, the Bible, we get an entirely different outlook, which should completely change the way we answer that question. The sexual revolution is not about sex; it is about redefining what it means to be human.

Transgenderism rests on the fundamental lie that sexuality is subjective. We can decide which sex we wish to be and/or be sexually involved with based on our feelings. Subjectivism says that all truth is relative, just as I spoke about earlier in this book. However, as we have already established, truth is not relative—it is absolute. Therefore, the truth about our sexuality cannot be subjective. Rather, it is *objective*. We are not in control of which sex we belong to.

There is an entertaining video which was released by the Washington Family Policy Council which illustrates the tension perfectly. A group of students are interviewed by a white male, who asks them questions such as "what if I told you I were a woman?" To this, they respond by affirming his position. He presses further, by asking "what about a Chinese woman?" To this, the students are a bit more hesitant to agree, but nevertheless, they ultimately do. Eventually, he gets to the point of asking, "What if I said I were a seven-year-old Chinese girl?" This demonstrates the difficulty that young people are having when they are faced with an objective reality but are being fed subjective lies about that reality. If we remove objective truth from culture, then the entire law of morality crumbles as well, soon afterward.

---

2. Watch the full Q&A here: https://www.youtube.com/watch?v=3eAmnzA6U-E.

Of course, it is important to note that very real psychological cases such as gender dysphoria do exist. Also, people do have same-sex attractions, and many do not wish to have them but feel as though they were "born" with these desires. These are very real instances, and these people deserve our love. However, affirming these desires, attractions, and thoughts is sinful and, as I will demonstrate, problematic and even harmful. So, for the sake of this chapter, we will be focusing on the false narratives and harmful behaviors of the transgender movement and current sexual revolution within America.

Drag Queen Story Hour

Something that is becoming more and more common in schools and throughout the internet is for transgender people to share their experiences with young children. The Washington Post featured a headline article in January of 2019 titled, "When drag queens lead children's story time, 'a lot of hugs'—and controversy—follow"[3] The story describes Raven Turner, also referred to as Raven Divine Cassadine, who is a transgender woman (a biological male who identifies as a female,) who visits schools to read stories to children and inform them on transgenderism. Raven reportedly commented, "the kids love it. Especially the girls; they thought I was a princess."

I came across a video on Facebook recently, however, that I found very interesting. It was titled, "Kids React to Drag." The video features a man named Reuben Kaye, a cabaret act who dresses in drag, and in this instance, visited young children in school. Some of the kids must have been no older than 5; regardless, Kaye asks them questions such as "do you think I look *normal?*" A little girl immediately responded confidently by saying, "No." To another girl, he asks, "Do you like what I'm wearing today?" She replies, " . . . Bit too much." A young boy asks Kaye, "Why do you have makeup and lipstick and glitter on?" The video proceeds to show

3. Bach, "drag queens," *Washington Post.*

that the children are developing an understanding that "everyone should be who they want to be." I do find it interesting that these young children, who have not experienced the world or the culture nearly as much as they will, still find it a bit perplexing that a grown man would be dressed in drag. Their minds are young and fragile and can be shaped in any way that adults choose. Even so, this type of content is abundant on apps such as TikTok; they will most likely encounter it one way or the other.

This is especially evident within the entertainment industry; children are targeted first. The narrative being pushed is that all types of sexuality apart from the Biblical view are normal and no longer something that needs to be argued. Take Pixar, for example. Disney and Pixar have been making incredible films for years, some of which are among my favorite movies of all time. The latest film by Pixar, "Onward," features an LGBTQ character known as Officer Specter. Though this character plays a minor role in the film, the producer stated that the character's inclusion felt organic, and that the fantasy setting of the film is meant to represent the real world. In other words, according to the producer, there is nothing fantastic or imaginative about LGBTQ sexuality. In a manner of speaking, this is correct! The narrative has successfully made its way into the culture and settled there, though more changes will undoubtedly arise before they get too comfortable. *Keep reading and see why this is already occurring.*

Another Pixar short focuses entirely on the main character "coming out" as openly gay. The short film, titled "Out," is only available on Disney+, Disney's streaming service. The story follows a man, Greg, who does not want to tell his parents he is gay, only to find out in the end that they always knew. Thus, he and his family embrace his same-sex relationship. Other instances like this include the latest Star Wars film, which features a same-sex kiss scene and a new Marvel movie, "The Eternals," which will have the first gay superhero. Disney's "High School Musical: The Series" featured a slow-dance between two male students, to which Sofia Wylie, one of the costars of the show, said "It's all become much more normalized, and I think that's really what the goal is." She is absolutely correct—the goal is, and has always been to *normalize* these narratives.

Disney is not alone in their messages, however. From children's cartoons like Arthur having a same-sex wedding for one of the characters, to Clifford the Big Red Dog introducing two lesbian characters, to HGTV airing an episode featuring a "throuple" (a polyamorous relationship, in this case between a man and two women). These ideals are presented as normal in the media, and children and teenagers are being fed the narrative first and foremost.

Going back to drag queen story hour, the Washington Post article then expounds on Raven's early life, and how he felt he did not belong in a male's body but was encouraged to "be who you are." For the transgender activists, "be who you are" often means the complete opposite. They challenge the notion that one's biology is correct; God must have got something wrong (if you hold to a theistic worldview, anyway,) because you are not in the right body. Therefore, you must change your appearance to fit your true personality, and even mutilate your body to do the same. Do you see how destructive of an idea this is? And we are only just learning how disastrous the consequences can be. This is the narrative being intentionally fed to children at the youngest ages possible. Why? Because the earlier they are exposed to it, the more status quo it becomes to the majority of children. And once a behavior or lifestyle is status quo, any opposition to it becomes "evil."

An independent journalist organization known as the Reality Report posted a video on Twitter of a transgender man dancing suggestively for a young girl sitting in a chair at a social gathering. While the girl sits alone among many adults, who laugh and cheer at the performance, the girl is given a provocative, up-close dance from the grown man. Of course, the sexualization of children is not merely limited to the transgender community, though it does seem to have been brought to the highest fruition as of the recent sexual revolution. Another similar video was posted to Twitter, featuring a pole-dancer performing for a group of elementary school students! These videos are just a glimpse into the stark realities which the redefinition and desacralization of sexuality has brought to our culture. With Instances such as these, why should we be surprised at Netflix for defending an original movie called "Cuties," which directly sexualizes young girls, over which there is much controversy.

Recently, a huge controversy erupted over a 7-year-old boy named James, who was forced by his mother to identify and dress as a girl, while his father was in complete opposition. The two parents were separated, and whenever James Younger was staying with his mother, she wanted him to be a girl, and he went along with it. The controversy sparked outrage and even a court case, from which James's father, Jeffrey Younger, was prohibited. He was not permitted to affirm his son's sex in any way, because his worldview did not fit the mainstream narrative. Instead, the court sided with James's mother, who opted for transitioning her son into a female—a procedure that includes pumping his body with hormonal sterilization and, in the most extreme cases, having surgery to reassign sexual reproductive organs.[4][5] Transgender activists ignore the fact that most gender-confused children end up growing out of their dysphoria, being that they are too young to understand it; instead, the trans-community insists on jumping to the extreme conclusion of affirming their psychological state and proceeding with potentially harmful long-term surgical procedures and medical treatments.

Is it not strange that, in the case of anorexia, for example, it would be considered malpractice to affirm one's psychological state? (Yes, you are in fact as skinny as you perceive yourself to be, despite the fact that you are severely malnourished in reality.) However, with transgenderism, it is considered hateful *not* to affirm that which does not correspond with reality. (Yes, you are in fact a female, despite having all the biological, anatomical, and genetic markers of being a male.) Yet, this is precisely what is happening, often without question, all across America. We are affirming lies about ourselves and encouraging children to do the same.

4. Bourne, "6-year-old boy," *Life Site News*.
5. Zraick, "Texas Father," *New York Times*.

> *Okay, but certainly there are undeniable truths about biological males and females which cannot be disputed. Not every truth is being abandoned, right?*

I beg to differ. Even the most fundamental aspects of male and female are being challenged by the notion of transgenderism. One of the most bizarre examples is menstruation. Many are arguing that men can have periods just like women. An article from the Daily Beast was titled, "Yes, Men Can Have Periods and We Need to Talk About Them." The subtitle reads, "Menstruation isn't just a "women's issue." It's time we opened up the conversation."[6] ScaryMommy.com, a public domain for mothers sharing pregnancy and motherhood advice and stories, featured a similar article titled, "Men Can Have Periods Too, And We Need To Normalize This."[7] Again, The Telegraph had an article saying, "Boys can have periods too, children to be taught in latest victory for transgender campaigners."[8] Now, many people recognize "National Period Day." One transgender rights activist posted on Twitter, "ANY GENDER CAN GET THEIR PERIOD" (repeated 7 times in the same thread). Make no mistake; if children are being told that male menstruation is normal, this is a serious problem.

The James Younger conflict was looked into by the Texas Attorney General's Office and the Texas Department of Family and Protective Services. Soon, a video surfaced during the Younger conflict which shed some light on the issue. The video begins with James saying, "I'm a girl."

> Jeffrey: "Who told you you were a girl?"
>
> James: "Mommy."
>
> Jeffrey: "When did she tell you you were a girl?"
>
> James: "Because I love girls."
>
> Jeffrey: "Oh, I see. So, Mommy told you you're a girl?"
>
> James: Nods, "Uh-huh."

6. Street, "Yes, Men Can Have Periods," *Daily Beast*.
7. Leventry, "Men Can Have Periods Too," *Scary Mommy*.
8. Horton, "Boys can have periods too," *The Telegraph*.

PART 3: INDOCTRINATION

The truth was soon revealed that James actually played a minor part in the overall narrative of his gender identity. Rather, it was his mother who was attempting to convince him that he was, in fact, in the wrong body, and was instead a girl named Luna. Even some websites such as Vox were affirming the false narrative of the child. An article from Vox was titled, "What the battle over a 7-year-old trans girl could mean for families nationwide."[9] The first two paragraphs of the article say this:

> Around age 3, Luna Younger started asking to wear dresses. Since the age of 5, she has insisted she is a girl. Now Luna is 7, and during court hearings, physicians, school staff, and family members have all testified that Luna has consistently, persistently identified as a girl.
>
> While Luna's mother respects her daughter's gender identity—letting her wear what she chooses, whether it's nail polish, dresses, or longer hair—Luna's father does not. He insists Luna is not transgender. These polarizing differences over how to raise and treat a child are why trans families and advocates, as well as conservatives, have been closely watching the custody battle over the Coppell, Texas, trans girl.

The article presupposes that the transgender ideals are true, and that the father is the enemy in the family.

Here is the good news: James reportedly did begin attending school as a boy; not as Luna. A Christian Post article details the information, as well as how his friends and family are fighting back against the harmful narrative of transgenderism as well.[10] The group, called SaveJames, said that they are "determined to get louder and now have thousands who will hold those Senators and Representatives accountable during the next election."

The Washington Post article about "drag queen story hour" explains the opposition that has been expressed concerning "drag queen story hour," describing a letter written by Allison Iversen, which says in one line, "Children are innocent little beings, and we, as a society, should be banding together to preserve that innocence."

9. Burns, "7-Year-Old Trans Girl," *Vox*
10. Showalter, "James Younger," *Christian Post.*

She makes a serious point: young children are being exposed to a culture of lies, which is harmful for several reasons.

Bathrooms and Locker Rooms

Recently, a video surfaced of a high school in Palatine which ruled that transgender students would be given unrestricted access to bathrooms and locker rooms of their choice. Julia Burca, a student at the school, was interviewed upon the passing of the new policy, and with visibly red, teary eyes, she said, "I feel uncomfortable that my privacy is being invaded. As I am a swimmer, I do change multiple times, naked, in front of other students in the locker room and I understand that the board has an obligation to all students, but I was hoping that they would go about this in a different way that would also accommodate students such as myself." Meanwhile, a male transgender student identified as Nova Maday who filed the lawsuit asking transgender students to be able to change in the common area of the girls' locker room, said, "It passed, it passed!" and "I'm ecstatic."

As was predicted by many in opposition to repealing acts such as HB2[11] to begin with, many sexual predators have already begun taking advantage of the transgender bathroom/locker room movement.[12] The case of Nova Maday is not the first instance in which this has occurred, however. A recent case in the Fourth Circuit Court ruled that a biological female who identified as a male was to be allowed to use the boys' restroom. The girl identified as a boy named G. G. The judge ruled, "G. G.'s birth-assigned sex, or so-called 'biological sex,' is female, but G. G.'s gender identity is male."[13] The law exists to protect citizens; now

---

11. The Public Facilities Privacy and Security Act, commonly referred to as "House Bill 2" is a North Carolina statute that compelled public facilities to only allow people to enter restrooms of the corresponding sex which their birth certificate identified. You can read the bill online here: https://www.ncleg.net/Sessions/2015E2/Bills/House/PDF/H2v1.pdf.

12. Turek, "Six Reasons," *Town Hall*.

13. *Gloucester County School Board v. G. G.*

it seems to merely attempt to satisfy them. And, ironically, this puts many other citizens in danger.

Unfortunately, the transgender narrative has not been introduced lightly. They immediately jumped to the most extreme conclusions. A BBC film called *Transgender Kids* featured a young woman known as Lou. She recounted, "The assumption from the outset was that if I said I was transgender, then I must be. Nobody at any point questioned my motives . . . [I] was very much told by the community that if you don't transition, you will self-harm and you will kill yourself. I became convinced that my options were transition or die." Our heart should go out to those who do seriously struggle with gender confusion or dysphoria. They need to know that they are loved and valued by their Creator, and their options certainly exceed those of "transition or die." A 2014 study discovered that 62.7 percent of people diagnosed with gender dysphoria suffer from psychiatric axis 1 disorders, or *mental illness*. That is to say they should receive treatment; they should not be forced into the conclusion that hormones and transition surgery must be the only answers.[14]

The transgender narrative actually proves to be *more* harmful in the long run, both emotionally and psychologically. The ideology suggests that if one's personality does not fit with the mainstream cultural expectation, then there must be something seriously wrong. In other words, you cannot be a girl and like hunting, fishing, wrestling, etc. (the activities most often associated with boys). Rather, you must be a boy trapped inside the body of a girl. I strongly push back against this; one reason is that I have never been into said activities, and I am a male. The transgender narrative, then, would tell me that there is something wrong with me. Ironically, by claiming to push back against the cultural expectations of gender roles, the transgender narrative reinforces them to a more extreme degree. Overall, studies have even shown that the transgender community is at a significantly high risk of suicide, particularly among people who are under the age of 21.[15]

14. Mazaheri et. al. "Psychiatric Axis 1," *Psychiatry Journal.*
15. Yüksel, et. al. "A Clinically Neglected Topic," *US National Library of*

Nancy Pearcey has a moving story to illustrate this point in her book, *Love Thy Body*. She describes a boy named Brandon, who, from childhood, was quiet, sensitive, and compliant. (I was the same way.) He sensed that he was different from most boys from an early age; while most boys liked sports and video games, Brandon did not take a particular interest in those activities. He eventually came to the heartbreaking conclusion, "God should have made me a girl."[16] We must understand that all children have differing personalities. Some may not fit the mold which society has carved out for them, and that is okay. They need to know that they are still loved and accepted *for who they are*. They should not be forced to change everything about them just to belong. Unfortunately, this is what the transgender narrative demands.

Introducing the Otherkin

The implications of transgenderism now stretch even further than gender. After all, once the snowball begins rolling, which the sexual revolution gave the first push to, it is almost impossible to stop the rapid growth, until something disastrous occurs. Many children and teenagers now self-identify as beings *other than human*. Jareth Nebula Argentum, 33, identifies as a *genderless alien*, and says this: "Being an alien is more than just my gender; it's how I am who I am. How my body reacts—it just feels 'alien.'"[17] Argentum proceeds to describe her appearance, with multiple tattoos. One of them, on the side of Argentum's head, resembles a circuit board. Argentum says of this tattoo, "it is representative of the inhuman or non-human

---

Medicine National Institutes of Health, 28–32. The study results read: "The incidence of suicide attempts, current suicidal thoughts, and lifetime suicidal thoughts were 29.8 percent, 9.2 percent, and 55.3 percent, respectively. In total, 76.7 percent of the suicide attempts occurred before the age of 21." Their conclusion is "Transsexual individuals present a high risk of suicide, particularly during adolescence. This finding may be considered a sign for taking action to prevent suicide when working with transgender individuals, particularly during adolescence."

16. Pearcey, *Love Thy Body*, 193.
17. Barcroft TV, "I've Transitioned Into An Alien," YouTube.com.

identified part of me." This is just one example; others have self-identified as monsters,[18] and many as merely animals. Vice even featured an article to this phenomenon, known as "trans-species" or "otherkin." The article describes a 15-year-old boy named Rivera:

> "I feel my selfhood to be discrete from this body. It's not inherently me—it's just a vehicle I'm operating. Plus, what does it mean to be human, anyway?" Riviera identifies as a dragon. He decided this 15 years ago after having what he describes as prophetic dreams of a past life . . . "I feel like there is a mix up between otherkins and furries in the media," he says. "For many otherkin, it's a quiet spiritual background to their lives, and not something that they can ever switch off."[19]

It is something they can *never* switch off? The article goes on to say that Rivera was asked if people in the trans-species community ever have sex with animals. Rivera responds by saying, "It is disgusting and illegal . . . Bestiality and zoophilia are treated with the same seriousness and abhorrence as wider society." However, same-sex marriage also used to be illegal, until the homosexual community fought for legalization. Who is to say the trans-species community will not begin to fight for bestiality rights? After all, as we have already seen, many pedophilia groups are already doing the same for pedophilia rights. The enforcement of this behavior already takes place in schools, of course. Many schools are refusing to inform parents when children are being taught LGBT ideals. In fact, the schools will unashamedly admit this, suggesting things like "teaching children about LGBT issues is not brainwashing—it equips them for life" (The Guardian).

This is a direct attack on the authority of God's Word. The devil is attempting to revoke the God-engraved image from humanity. Again, to quote Mike Adams, this is not about where the transgendered pee; it is about changing society's standards, in this case, at the expense of the privacy of many young people. Postmodernism has twisted the truth about sex and gender and created an infinitely

18. Barcroft TV, "I'm Becoming a Genderless Monster," YouTube.com
19. Graves-Browne, "What It Means To Be Trans Species," *Vice*.

malleable version that is completely subjective and opposed to God's Word. Why should any of this surprise us, though? J. Budziszewski writes, "The shape of human life must be transformed. All of the assumptions of normal sexuality must be dissolved: marriage, family, innocence, purity, childhood—all must be called into question, even if it means pulling the world around their ears."[20] Budziszewski is a professor of government and philosophy at the University of Texas, Austin, who questions the idea that moral truths are unknowable. In order to ensure thriving future generations of children, we must affirm that objective morals *do* exist, and absolute truths about what it means to be human *do* exist.

There is a necessary balance, however, between grace and truth. I believe Dr. Michael Brown evaluates the argument wonderfully in his book *Can You Be Gay and Christian?* He says this:

> You are not defined by your attractions, and you are not a slave to your desires. You can even live without sex or be single (if that is God's will, although he has the power to change your attractions), but you cannot live without Him. And so, rather than focusing on whether you are gay or bi or tans (or something else), why not focus on finding that one glorious, beautiful pearl of great price, that incredible, mind-boggling hidden treasure in the field: Jesus, the Lord and Savior.[21]

That is the key—the gospel message. Though Jesus does not accept our sinful desires, he accepts us and offers us forgiveness and redemption from them. God does not change with the culture; he will not change his mind to fit the narrative of our time. He will, however, hold his promise that anyone who calls on his name will be saved (Romans 10:13).

Pushing back against lies and demonic forces within the culture is not an easy task, especially when the majority has followed suit. However, as Christians, we cannot compromise. God's word remains authoritative, and His truth is the only thing that can deflect the attacks of the enemy.

20. Budziszewski, *What We Can't Not Know,* 153.
21. Brown, *Can You Be Gay and Christian?* 221.

Finally, be strong in the Lord and in the strength of His might. Put on the full armor of God, so that you will be able to stand firm against the schemes of the devil. For our struggle is not against flesh and blood, but against the rulers, against the powers, against the world forces of this darkness, against the spiritual forces of wickedness in the heavenly places. Therefore, take up the full armor of God, so that you will be able to resist in the evil day, and having done everything, to stand firm. Stand firm therefore, having girded your loins with truth, and having put on the breastplate of righteousness, and having shod your feet with the preparation of the gospel of peace; in addition to all, taking up the shield of faith with which you will be able to extinguish all the flaming arrows of the evil one. And take the helmet of salvation, and the sword of the Spirit, which is the word of God.

With all prayer and petition pray at all times in the Spirit, and with this in view, be on the alert with all perseverance and petition for all the saints. (Ephesians 6:10–18)

Recommended Resources

Love Thy Body: Answering Hard Questions about Life and Sexuality by Nancy Pearcey

Can You Be Gay and Christian? Responding with Love and Truth to Hard Questions About Homosexuality by Michael L. Brown, PhD

Correct, Not Politically Correct: How Same Sex Marriage Hurts Everyone by Frank Turek

When Harry Became Sally: Responding to the Transgender Movement by Ryan T. Anderson

A Practical Guide to Culture: Helping the Next Generation Navigate Today's World by Brett Kunkle and John Stonestreet

Is God Anti-Gay? by Sam Allberry

Same-Sex Marriage (Thoughtful Response): A Thoughtful Approach to God's Design for Marriage by John Stonestreet and Sean McDowell

Conclusion

The Vitality of a Biblical Foundation

THE LIES OF THE culture seem more and more pervasive (and persuasive) every day. Our hearts should be breaking for our lost culture. They need the gospel too. It is crucial that we disciple young people to know that they are in fact lies. Roughly 75 percent of students who grow up in church end up walking away from the church after high school. That is 3 out of every 4 students! Why?

One of the biggest contributing factors is the church itself. We are not discipling like we should be in many American churches. Too many churches, with the looming threat of the progressive culture, have thus compromised and bowed to the bullying. In turn, many of the horrors thriving in society exist with the consent of the church. We are not making a strong enough effort to combat the lies with truth. So, when students are faced with the lies in the culture, they are unable to discern what is true, or defend why they believe what they believe. In turn, they end up becoming indoctrinated by false teachers and abandoning the church (and thus, possibly their faith as well.)

The challenge, as we have discussed, in the age of media is the propensity to resort to a quick internet search when it comes to the hard questions. Children and teenagers today are growing up with the ease-of-access to information. The downside to this is, as we have seen, the narratives being pushed within the media. In fact, though major search engines claim to display the aggregate search information, this only proves the importance of finding reputable sources. In other words, merely searching for a question online does not guarantee that one will find a true answer by the first result that shows up. Also, the internet is an open domain where anyone can share ideas and information; many conservative and evangelical voices are often censored, however. There is an urgency in teaching children where to find the right answers and how to discern falsity.

But what is so harmful about redefining some concepts?

It is not as simple as merely "redefining" concepts and leaving it at that—this is a direct attack on the authority of God's Word. Why? Once the foundation is destroyed, the rest of the structure crumbles. We are seeing this happen first-hand already across the globe. It is just as Paul warned Timothy: "For the time will come when they will not endure sound doctrine; but wanting to have their ears tickled, they will accumulate for themselves teachers in accordance to their own desires" (2 Timothy 4:3). This is precisely what is occurring now; people are abandoning truth for lies in an attempt to eradicate the truth of Scripture from the world completely.

Is it any coincidence that some of the fundamental ideas of God's Word are being completely perverted? Truth, Jesus, marriage, sexuality, the sanctity of life; these are just a few topics which the culture has redefined. It has never been more important to disciple children so that they may be able to discern the lies which are so prevalent in our society.

Culture says: truth is relative. You can believe what you want.[1]

---

1. ...But if you disagree with the mainstream narrative, you are an intolerant bigot. Notice that the ones who are fighting for "tolerance" are often the most intolerant. They want tolerance, but only for *their* viewpoint.

CONCLUSION

God's Word says: Truth is absolute. There is one truth, and his name is Jesus (John 14:6; see also Romans 1:18, 2:6–8, 2 Thessalonians 2:11–12).

Culture says: marriage can be whatever you want it to be.

God's Word says: Marriage is created by God to be a monogamous, covenant relationship between a man and a woman, and sex was created to be shared within this context alone (Genesis 2:24, Matthew 19:5).

Culture says: sexuality is whatever you want it to be.

God's Word says: God created humanity in His image as male and female (Genesis 1:27).

Culture says: Abortion is a woman's right; a preborn baby is just a clump of cells.

God's Word says: The baby's life is sacred, from conception (Psalm 139:13). Abortion is the immoral act of killing a preborn child.

Truth will always make enemies, simply because it is truth. Paul experienced this opposition as well, when he said in Galatians 4:16, "So have I become your enemy by telling you the truth?" Children will also face opposition, and ridicule as well, for standing firm in God's name.

Who Let These Monsters In?

Several years ago, author and apologist Frank Turek wrote an article titled, "Country a Mess? Blame the Church." In it, he argues this:

> Believers are God's ambassadors here on earth, called to be salt and light in the world and to the world. When we follow our calling, individuals are transformed and societies with them. Our country is failing because too many believers have abandoned this calling... Is it any wonder

why those areas of our culture now seem so Godless? Take the influence of God out, and that's what you get.²

The increasing Godlessness and postmodernism of society began to come to a head when the church began to abandon the fundamentals of the faith. In an effort to be more inclusive, we in turn neglect the Kingdom and thus the church—and nation—fall into a state of apostasy from the truth. The secularization of America is a result of many issues overarching one central error: the removal of God from the public square. Too many churches, even, have abandoned reason and truth for emotionalism and feel-good messages. As a result, the monsters which once lingered in the closet have made their dwelling in every room of the house. They creep around in classrooms, media, churches, courtrooms, literature, and as we have seen, everywhere on the internet. The monsters of Satan's army are on the offensive. Turek goes on:

> "So what?" you say. "Who cares about morality and God?"
>
> That's exactly the problem: Who does care? When the church separates from society, it takes its moral influence with it. But respect for the moral principles upon which our nation was founded—life, liberty and the pursuit of happiness—is essential to its survival. Our founders knew this.

If the church does not stand up, who will? Radical laws, the deconstruction of marriage, political correctness as a religion, sexual immorality, celebratory abortion, the banning of the Bible, pornographic content saturating the internet, and a society which praises these things are merely the beginning of the lawlessness to follow a nation without God. The church must become more active at each of these levels, and parents must not only be on defense for the sake of their children, but on offense for the sake of God's Word. The Christian message is one of redemption. There is always hope for revival.

Many of the monsters we have discussed have been allowed to enter in with the consent of the church. When the world

2. Turek, "Country a Mess?" *Town Hall.*

abandons the truth of the Bible, its words are considered foreign, legendary, mythical, outdated, and irrelevant. Therefore, when we are faced with the realities of spiritual warfare which it promises, we brush them off as nothing more than sheer happenstance and, if anything, the so-called progression of the culture. In reality, a world that no longer believes in a real, invisible enemy is blinded to his attacks.

Do Not Bow

Most of the false narratives and lies which I have addressed in this book are no longer being argued for but have become the status quo. And as C. S. Lewis said, "The most dangerous ideas in a society are not the ones that are argued, but the ones that are assumed." It takes boldness to stand for Christ. In fact, if the mainstream media were to read this book, there would be a lot of backlash. Even with the evidence for the harmful consequences of things such as pornography, people do not want to accept the truth of God's Word, often for that very reason—because it is His Word.

The world is becoming increasingly hostile to Christians. Jesus promised that this would happen. He said, "If the world hates you, you know that it has hated Me before it hated you." (John 15:18). Expect opposition, but do not bow to the narratives that are being fed through the culture. The enemy knows that if he can lead children astray, he has won. After all, they are the next generation. We cannot let that happen. We cannot bow to the schemes of the enemy to redefine sexuality, redefine what is morally good, and blot out the truth of Jesus from being proclaimed. Stand for truth. Stand for Jesus.

Parents are the gatekeepers of the household. God has put them in place to lead and disciple children. I hope that this book has exposed some of the realities of the many lies they are being fed and exposed to. The world is evil, but God is good. The only thing that can truly melt the stone heart of a perverse culture is the sweet, saving grace of Christ. Only the beauty of a life worth living to glorify the one who gave it breath will expose the beauty of a life which cannot yet sustain itself. Only the realization of the careful design of humans to flourish for the purpose of praising our maker and enjoying Him abundantly will make evident the purpose of His design to begin with. Only the love of a God who is both merciful and just can replace the monsters in the closet with grace and truth in the heart.

Appendix

Answers to Common Objections/Questions

THERE IS NO DOUBT that many of the points raised in this book will create room for objections. Naturally, we should be prepared to answer the hard questions which teenagers and children will have about difficult topics. Here are some of the most common questions and objections I encounter (with regards to what was covered in this book) and some brief answers to them.

Pornography

I am not morally opposed to pornography; why should I care?

Because porn is more than a moral issue. It is harmful both to its actors and its viewers. Horror stories consistently surface about the terrible experience porn creates for actors. Porn actors are often drugged or encouraged to get drunk so that they will be able to suppress the emotional and spiritual reality of sex in which they engage. Also, porn consumption, according to psychological studies (cited in the footnotes), can lead to unrealistic sexual beliefs and values, an over-focus or obsession on sex, sex addiction, sexually aggressive behaviors, sexually permissive behaviors, an earlier interest in having sex, promiscuity, questions about their own body, questions about their sexual performance, behavior problems, depression, and bonding issues with others, including parents. In other words, *porn hurts everyone.*

I am a porn addict.
It is too late for me to change.

It is never too late to change; you just have to be willing to seek help. The first step in getting well is admitting that you are sick. The fact that you are aware of the problem is a step in the right direction. It would be wrong to accept that as part of who you are because we are not defined by our sinful desires. Porn is harmful and sinful. But there is good news. You may feel like you are in captivity to sin, but Jesus came to set the captives free (Luke 4:18). In addition, Satan does not have rule over your body; God promises us a way out of every temptation (1 Corinthians 10:13). Seek counseling immediately if you feel addicted to pornography; do not accept your current state. Christ calls us to new life, which involves turning from the old. It is never too late to seek guidance on how to do that.

Abortion

You should not impose your religious view of abortion on people.

As I said, this is not *my* view. I did not decide that abortion is wrong. I do, however, *recognize* that it is wrong, because taking the innocent life of a human being is murder. Secondly, that is not a religious belief. It just happens to be consistent with what the Bible says about the sanctity of life. In other words, an atheist can be pro-life.

APPENDIX: ANSWERS TO COMMON OBJECTIONS/QUESTIONS

Okay, but it is not a human; it is just a clump of cells.

I am often surprised that so many people still hold to this objection. With the rise of ultrasound technology, the truth is undeniable. Within the early stages of development, we can clearly see that the fetus has eyes, fingers, toes, and a heartbeat. From the moment of conception, an entirely new set of DNA is given to the child. He or she does not gain any more genetic information from that point forward in life. The unborn baby needs only time, air, water, and food to reach adulthood; these are the same four basic requirements of adults.

Besides, even if there is uncertainty as to what it might be, we should always err on the side of life; if your child were missing, you would not take a pitchfork and start jabbing it into bushes to see if he or she is in there, for the risk of killing them. Likewise, even if we were somewhat uncertain if a fetus were really a human life, why would we not take the safest road and protect it anyways?

Lastly, if it is just a clump of cells, or a part of the woman's body, that is an awfully unique clump of cells. No other part of a woman's body has its own set of DNA and will one day be able to walk, talk, love, and reproduce. Why else was the argument for abortion "safe, legal, and *rare*" for so many years? Why should abortion be rare if there is nothing immoral about it?

Abortion is a woman's right. Roe v. Wade made that certain.

No one has the right to take an innocent life. This is why some may phrase the argument like "I am not pro-abortion; I am pro-*choice*." That is what it means to be pro-choice. You are claiming that a woman has the right to *choose abortion*. If the freedom to choose is of utmost importance, then who are we to discriminate against *any* choice, including racist, sexist, bigoted choices? (Interestingly, some of the reasons for choosing abortion fall into these categories. For example, the vast majority of babies diagnosed with

Down Syndrome are aborted, and black babies are aborted at a much higher rate than white babies.)

Secondly, the argument for Roe v Wade was made for Plessy v Ferguson as well, which legalized segregation. The law does not determine right and wrong—it seeks to recognize it, but unfortunately bad laws can exist.

It may be human, but it is not a person.

Every time in history that the personhood of a human being was revoked, there were disastrous consequences. After all, this was the same argument made against Jews in the holocaust during WWII. It was the same argument made against African American slaves as well—the idea being that because they are not "persons," they are not deserving of the same rights and protections as the rest of American citizens. What makes abortion unique in comparison even to those examples is that the unborn baby has no way to defend his or herself, whereas African American slaves, for example, were able to rebel. It is the duty of the people to protect those who cannot protect themselves.

What about rape and incest?

Before we even address the question, it must be asserted that rape and incest situations are heartbreaking, and the victims of these crimes deserve our love and support. Those who commit the crimes should be punished by the extent of the law. It cannot be ignored, however, that oftentimes these cases are appealed to justify abortion at large. Abortion advocates often take the marginal cases in order to argue for the standard. The fact of the matter is that rape and incest account for *just 1 percent* of abortion cases in America.

Secondly, one act of injustice does not justify another act of injustice. The baby should not be punished for a crime he or she did not commit. As Frank Turek and Norman Geisler point out, "the murder of an innocent human being to relieve the suffering of another is never justified."[1] After all, we do not murder the children who have already been born whose mothers are the victims of rape. Likewise, there is no difference between them, anyone else, or the unborn baby, that would justify taking an innocent life, regardless of the circumstances by which they were created.

Sexuality

Children should not be forced to stick to their gender assigned at birth.

First, gender is not *assigned* at birth; it is *recognized*. We recognize that there are distinct differences between the two sexes, male and female. When the definition of gender becomes virtually limitless, we ultimately consider the biological markers irrelevant. But they are very relevant.

Second, most children who experience gender confusion at a young age grow out of those feelings. They are children, after all! There is a reason that the age of consent and right to vote are 18 years old, and that the legal age to purchase tobacco and alcohol is 21 years old. Children's minds are still developing. Why should we allow them to choose to change their entire identity at such a young, naïve age? Remember that gender changes typically involve puberty blockers as early as 8 years old, cross-sex hormones as early as 14, and surgical genital reassignment sometimes as early as 17 years old!

Gender is not the same as sex.

When we isolate gender from sex, we are claiming that gender is solely in the mind. Again, this makes the biological markers ultimately irrelevant. A doctor would not affirm the psychological state of someone with anorexia because it contradicts reality.

---

1. Turek and Geisler, *Legislating Morality*, 168.

Likewise, we should not affirm a psychological state of gender which contradicts reality. These are subjective claims about reality, which are a matter of opinion; we must base our reasoning off *objective* reality, which is unchangeable. Identity has been split between biology and ideology. Thus, gender identity has been separated from sex, though this was not always be case.

Some people are intersex.

It is true that some people are born seemingly with both female and male organs, but it is important to remember that this is the exception and not the rule. The medical anomaly, known as hermaphroditism, is very rare. But again, we should not formulate society based on exceptions. In fact, in most cases of intersex, the biological indicators do exist, but are more difficult to determine. As a result, most people who fall under this category end up choosing one sex, rather than living with two.

Secondly, this objection actually has nothing to do with transgenderism, for example, because transgenderism is a totally different issue. It is the psychological state of "identifying" as the opposite gender, or as we have seen, beings other than human altogether.

What about tolerance?

We all recognize that not all behaviors or lifestyles deserve tolerance. The actions of a rapist should not be tolerated. This is why it is important to remember that we are not discriminating against *people*, but *behaviors*. The transgender narrative is harmful and false, and we need to speak the truth in love.

Secondly, Jesus did not affirm all lifestyles. He calls us to a life of repentance and putting off the old in order to follow him. Part of being a Christian is about what we are willing to give up to follow Christ. It is important to note that love does not require approval. We should not approve of immoral acts. Likewise, it would be unloving to approve of every behavior and lifestyle a person affirms for the sake of tolerance. The Bible makes clear that sexuality is designed by God as male and female (Genesis 1:27). Sex was created to be shared within the context a monogamous union between a man and a woman, known as marriage. Anything outside of this is sexual immorality (Mark 7:21, 1 Corinthians 6:18, Hebrews 13:4, 1 Thessalonians 4:3–5). Jesus does not affirm our sinful desires; he reorients them in accordance with his will.

This does not mean we should not love people who hold to a lifestyle that is wrong; on the contrary, it would be *unloving not* to tell them the truth. With children and teenagers, it is more important than ever to speak the truth in love on these topics. We will never have *all* the answers, but we know the one who does.

Bibliography

Adeane, Ant. "Blue Whale: What is the truth behind an online 'suicide challenge'?" *BBC News,* January 13, 2019. https://www.bbc.com/news/blogs-trending-46505722

Anderson, Karen. "FBI Warns Parents About Sextortion Online." *CBS Boston,* February 28, 2012. https://boston.cbslocal.com/2012/02/28/fbi-warns-parents-about-sextortion-online/#parenting

Bach, Trevor. "When drag queens lead children's story time, 'a lot of hugs' — and controversy — follow." *Washington Post,* January 25, 2019. https://www.washingtonpost.com/national/when-drag-queens-lead-childrens-story-time-lots-of-hugs—and-controversy—follow/2019/01/25/a47ab49c-2002-11e9-9145-3f74070bbdb9_story.html

Baker, Felicity and William Bor. "Can Music Preference Indicate Mental Health Status in Young People?" *Sage Journals:* Australian Psychiatry. (2008). https://doi.org/10.1080/10398560701879589

Barcroft TV. "I'm Becoming a Genderless Monster | HOOKED ON THE LOOK," YouTube.com, April 2019. Accessed December 31, 2019. https://www.youtube.com/watch?v=TkmozCseus4.

———. "I've Transitioned Into An Alien | HOOKED ON THE LOOK," YouTube.com, June 2019. https://www.youtube.com/watch?v=409MhK-hhXo Accessed December 31, 2019.

Bourne, Lisa. "6-year-old boy forced to live as a girl while mom threatens dad for not going along." *Life Site News,* November 28, 2018. https://www.lifesitenews.com/news/6-year-old-boy-forced-to-live-as-a-girl-while-mom-threatens-dad-for-not-goi.

Bozell, L. Brent. "Democrats on Sex and Children." *Media Research Center,* October 12, 2006. http://archive.mrc.org/BozellColumns/newscolumn/2006/col20061012.asp.

Brandt, Richard. "Google divulges numbers at I/O: 20 billion texts, 93 million selfies and more." *Silicon Valley Business Journal*, June 25, 2014. https://www.bizjournals.com/sanjose/news/2014/06/25/google-divulges-numbers-at-i-0-20-billion-texts-93.html

Bridges, Ana J., et al. "Aggression and Sexual Behavior in Best Selling Pornography Videos: A Content Analysis Update." *Violence Against Women*, 16(10) (2010). https://doi.org/10.1177/1077801210382866

Brown, Michael L. *Can You Be Gay and Christian? Responding with Love and Truth to Hard Questions About Homosexuality*. Lake Mary: Front Line, 2014.

Budziszewski, J. *What We Can't Not Know*. Dallas: Spence, 2003.

Burns, Katelyn. "What the battle over a 7-year-old trans girl could mean for families nationwide." *Vox*, November 11, 2019.

CBS News. "'Momo Challenge' nearly deadly for family, California mother says." February 28, 2019. https://www.cbsnews.com/news/momo-challenge-nearly-deadly-for-family-california-mother-says/.

Collins, Gary. *Christian Counseling. A Comprehensive Guide*. 3rd ed. Nashville: Thomas Nelson, 2007.

Diaz, Pauline. "The role of schools in bridging the abortion information gap." *Safe2Choose.org*, March 12, 2019. https://safe2choose.org/news/role-of-schools-abortion-information-gap/.

Fight the New Drug. "How Mainstream Porn Fuels Child Exploitation and Sex Trafficking." *Fight the New Drug*, December 9, 2019. https://fightthenewdrug.org/inside-the-industry-where-child-exploitation-pornography-and-sex-trafficking-collide/.

———. "10 Ex-Porn Performers Reveal the Brutal Truth Behind Their Most Popular Scenes." *Fight the New Drug*, September 3, 2019. https://fightthenewdrug.org/10-porn-stars-speak-openly-about-their-most-popular-scenes/.

———. "One-Sided Orgasms: Pornhub's Most Popular Videos Don't Show Mutual Pleasure." *Fight the New Drug*, April 3, 2019. https://fightthenewdrug.org/largest-porn-site-most-watched-videos-dont-show-mutual-pleasure/.

———. "Can You Guess 2018's Most Viewed Categories On The Largest Porn Site?" *Fight the New Drug*, July 9, 2019. https://fightthenewdrug.org/pornhub-visitors-in-2018-and-review-of-top-searches/.

———. "Google Removes Dozens of Kid-Friendly Apps Because of Porn Malware." *Fight the New Drug*, January 27, 2018. https://fightthenewdrug.org/google-removes-kids-apps-because-of-porn/

———. "What's the Average Age of a Child's First Exposure to Porn?" *Fight the New Drug*, January 28, 2020. https://fightthenewdrug.org/real-average-age-of-first-exposure/

Freitas, Donna. *The Happiness Effect: How Social Media is Driving a Generation to Appear Perfect at Any Cost*. New York: Oxford University Press, 2017.

Gallop. "Gay and Lesbian Rights."

BIBLIOGRAPHY

Geisler, Norman, and Frank Turek. *Legislating Morality: Is It Wise? Is It Legal? Is It Possible?* Eugene: Wipf & Stock, 1998.

Gloucester County School Board v. G. G. United States Court of Appeals for the Fourth Circuit. No. 15-2056. decided: April 19, 2016.

Graves-Browne, Eliza. "What It Means To Be Trans Species," *Vice*, April 2016. https://www.vice.com/en_us/article/yvwknv/what-does-it-mean-to-be-trans-species.

Harvard Mental Health Letter. "How addiction hijacks the brain." July 2011. https://www.health.harvard.edu/newsletter_article/how-addiction-hijacks-the-brain Accessed July 3, 2019.

Hennessy, Michael, et al. "Estimating the longitudinal association between adolescent sexual behavior and exposure to sexual media content." *Journal of Sex Research* 46 (6) (2009). doi: 10.1080/00224490902898736.

Horton, Helena. "Boys can have periods too, children to be taught in latest victory for transgender campaigners." *The Telegraph*, December 16, 2018. https://www.telegraph.co.uk/news/2018/12/16/boys-can-have-periods-schoolchildren-taught-latest-victory-transgender/.

Huerta, Danny. "Seven Strategies to Combat Teen Porn Use." *Focus on The Family*, August 14, 2018. https://www.focusonthefamily.com/parenting/seven-strategies-to-combat-teen-porn-use/.

———. "How Pornography Affects a Teen Brain." *Focus on the Family*, August 14, 2008. https://focusonthefamily.com/parenting/how-pornography-affects-a-teen-brain/.

J. Raghuram et al, "Effects of Sexual Advertising on Customer Buying Decisions." *IOSR Journal of Business Engagement* 7 (2015). http://www.iosrjournals.org/iosr-jbm/papers/Vol17-issue7/Version-3/B017730511.pdf.

Keller, Michael H. and Gabriel J.X. Dance. "The Internet Is Overrun With Images of Child Sexual Abuse. What Went Wrong?" *New York Times*, September 29, 2019. https://www.nytimes.com/interactive/2019/09/28/us/child-sex-abuse.html.

Kim, Eun Kyung. "Vivid Time Lapse Shows How Photoshop Makes Models Picture Perfect." *Today*, May 5, 2015. https://www.today.com/style/photoshop-videos-show-reality-picture-perfect-images-t19421.

Kleinman, Alexis. "Porn Sites Get More Visitors Each Month Than Netflix, Amazon and Twitter Combined." *Huffpost*, December 6, 2017. https://www.huffpost.com/entry/internet-porn-stats_n_3187682.

Lane, Frederick S. *Obscene Profits: The Entrepreneurs of Pornography in the Cyber Age*. New York: Routledge, 2000.

Layden, M. A. *Committee on Commerce, Science, and Transportation, Subcommittee on Science and Space, U.S. Senate*. "Hearing on the Brain Science Behind Pornography Addiction." November 18, 2004.

Lenhart, Amanda. "Teens, Social Media & Technology Overview 2015." *Pew Research Center*, April 9, 2015. https://www.pewresearch.org/internet/2015/04/09/teens-social-media-technology-2015/.

Leventry, Amber. "Men Can Have Periods Too, And We Need To Normalize This." *Scary Mommy,* April 17, 2019. https://www.scarymommy.com/men-can-have-periods-too/.

Lewis, Sophie. "Police issue warning to parents after "Momo Challenge" resurfaces." *CBS News,* February 28, 2019. https://www.cbsnews.com/news/momo-challenge-resurfaces-police-issue-warning-to-parents/.

Live Action. "As defund debate hits, Live Action exposes Planned Parenthood's prenatal care deception." January 23, 2017. https://www.liveaction.org/defund-debate-hits-live-action-exposes-planned-parenthoods-prenatal-care-deception/.

Luscombe, Belinda. "Porn and the Threat to Virility." *Time* (2016).

Mazaheri, Azadeh et. al. "Psychiatric Axis 1 Comorbidities among Patients with Gender Dysphoria." *Psychiatry Journal* (2014). doi: 10.1155/2014/971814.

McLean, Siân A. et al, "Photoshopping the selfie: Self photo editing and photo investment are associated with body dissatisfaction in adolescent girls." *International Journal of Eating Disorders* 48(8) (2015). https://doi.org/10.1002/eat.22449.

Mineo, Liz. "A warning on homeschooling." *The Harvard Gazette,* May 15, 2020. https://news.harvard.edu/gazette/story/2020/05/law-school-professor-says-there-may-be-a-dark-side-of-homeschooling/.

Newberry, Julie. "Viewing Child Abuse Images: Pedophile or Addicted to Porn?" *Psychreg,* August 8, 2017. https://www.psychreg.org/paedophile-addicted-porn/.

O'Donnell, Erin. "The Risks of Homeschooling." *Harvard Magazine,* May 2020. https://www.harvardmagazine.com/2020/05/right-now-risks-homeschooling.

O'Neill, Essena. "Dear 12 Year Old Self (re-upload)," YouTube, November 8, 2015. Accessed December 11, 2019. https://www.youtube.com/watch?v=CRXZXIKd-hA.

Owens, Alice. "My Rape Convinced Me That Campus Hookup Culture is Really Messed Up." *Verily,* July 6, 2015. https://verilymag.com/2015/07/sexual-assault-campus-hookup-culture-date-rape.

Paul, Pamela. *Pornified: How Pornography Is Transforming Our Lives, Our Relationships, and Our Families.* New York: Henry Holt & Co. 2007.

Pearcey, Nancy. *Love Thy Body: Answering Hard Questions About Life and Sexuality.* Grand Rapids, MI: Baker, 2018.

Perkins, Tony. "Fighting Abortion—The Measure of a Just Society." *Answers in Genesis,* October 1, 2010. https://answersingenesis.org/sanctity-of-life/abortion/fighting-abortion-the-measure-of-a-just-society/.

Reinke, Tony. *12 Ways Your Phone Is Changing You.* Wheaton, IL: Crossway, 2017.

Ryan, Sloan. "I'm A 37-Year-Old Mom & I Spent Seven Days Online as an 11-Year-Old Girl. Here's What I Learned." *Medium,* December 13, 2019. https://medium.com/@sloane_ryan/im-a-37-year-old-mom-i-spent-seven-days-online-as-an-11-year-old-girl-here-s-what-i-learned-9825e81c8e7d.

Séguin, Léa J. et. al. "Consuming Ecstasy: Representations of Male and Female Orgasm in Mainstream Pornography." *Journal of Sex Research* (2018). doi: 10.1080/00224499.2017.1332152.

Showalter, Brandon. "James Younger, 7-y-o child at center of Save James case, goes to school as boy for first time." *Christian Post,* November 7, 2019. https://www.christianpost.com/news/james-younger-7-y-o-child-at-center-of-save-james-case-goes-to-school-as-boy-for-first-time.html.

Silver, Laura. "Smartphone Ownership Is Growing Rapidly Around the World, but Not Always Equally." *Pew Research Center,* February 5, 2019. https://www.pewresearch.org/global/2019/02/05/smartphone-ownership-is-growing-rapidly-around-the-world-but-not-always-equally/.

Sorokowski, P. et al. "Selfie posting behaviors are associated with narcissism among men." *Personality and Individual Differences.* 85 (2015).

Street, Zoyander. "Yes, Men Can Have Periods and We Need To Talk About Them." *Daily Beast,* July 12, 2017. https://www.thedailybeast.com/yes-men-can-have-periods-and-we-need-to-talk-about-them.

Szulman, Jennifer. "Pornography actor opens up 'Porn University' for aspiring adult performers." *Daily News,* October 6, 2015. https://www.nydailynews.com/news/world/porn-university-opens-aspiring-adult-film-performers-article-1.2387263

Turek, Frank. *Correct, Not Politically Correct: How Same Sex Marriage Hurts Everyone.* Charlotte: MorningStar, 2011.

———. "Country a Mess? Blame the Church." *Town Hall,* July 15, 2009. https://townhall.com/columnists/frankturek/2009/07/15/country-a-mess—blame-the-church-n732477.

———. "Six Reasons North Carolina Got it Right." *Town Hall,* March 30, 2016. https://townhall.com/columnists/frankturek/2016/03/30/six-reasons-north-carolina-got-it-right-n2141010.

University of Southern California Department of Nursing. "America's Sex Education: How We Are Failing Our Students." September 18, 2017. https://nursing.usc.edu/blog/americas-sex-education/.

Weinberg, Martin S. et. al., "Pornography, normalization and empowerment," *Archives of Sexual Behavior* 39(6) (2010). doi: 10.1007/s10508-009-9592-5.

Weiser, Eric B. "#Me: Narcissism and its facets as predictors of selfie-posting frequency." *Personality and Individual Differences* 86 (2015).

Whelan, Ed. "Slate's Noah on Graham and Ginsburg: Wrong Again." *National Review,* September 30, 2005. https://www.nationalreview.com/bench-memos/slates-noah-graham-and-ginsburg-wrong-again-ed-whelan/.

Wolak, Janis, David Finkelhor, Kimberly J. Mitchell, Michele L. Ybarra. "Online 'Predators' and their Victims: Myths, Realities and Implications for Prevention and Treatment." PDF File. *University of New Hampshire.* http://www.unh.edu/ccrc/pdf/Am%20Psy%202-08.pdf.

———. (2008) *American Psychologist,* 63. Copyright APA. http://content.apa.org/journals/amp.

Wolf, Michelle. "Joke Show." *Netflix,* 2019.

Wolf, Naomi. "Casual Sex Finds a Cool New Position." *The Sunday Times*, January 12, 2003. http://209.157.64.200/focus/f-news/821113/posts.

Woods, John. "Jamie is 13 and Hasn't Even Kissed a Girl. But He's Now On the Sex Offender Register after Online Porn Warped His Mind." *Daily Mail*, April 25, 2012. https://www.dailymail.co.uk/news/article-2135203/Jamie-13-kissed-girl-But-hes-Sex-Offender-Register-online-porn-warped-mind-.html.

Yüksel, Şahika, et al. "A Clinically Neglected Topic: Risk of Suicide in Transgender Individuals." *US National Library of Medicine National Institutes of Health* 54(1) (2017) doi: 10.5152/npa.2016.10075.

Zillmann, Dolf. (2000). Influence of Unrestrained Access to Erotica on Adolescents' and Young Adults' Dispositions Toward Sexuality. *Journal of Adolescent Health* 27(2) (2000). doi: https://doi.org/10.1016/S1054-139X(00)00137-3.

Zraick, Karen. "Texas Father Says 7-Year-Old Isn't Transgender, Igniting a Politicized Outcry." *New York Times*, October 28, 2019. https://www.nytimes.com/2019/10/28/us/texas-transgender-child.html.

www.ingramcontent.com/pod-product-compliance
Lightning Source LLC
Chambersburg PA
CBHW070047100426
42734CB00039B/2183